1,000,000 Books

are available to read at

www.ForgottenBooks.com

Read online
Download PDF
Purchase in print

1 MONTH OF FREE READING

at

www.ForgottenBooks.com

By purchasing this book you are eligible for one month membership to ForgottenBooks.com, giving you unlimited access to our entire collection of over 1,000,000 titles via our web site and mobile apps.

To claim your free month visit: www.forgottenbooks.com/free243427

* Offer is valid for 45 days from date of purchase. Terms and conditions apply.

English
Français
Deutsche
Italiano
Español
Português

www.forgottenbooks.com

Mythology Photography **Fiction**
Fishing Christianity **Art** Cooking
Essays Buddhism Freemasonry
Medicine **Biology** Music **Ancient Egypt** Evolution Carpentry Physics
Dance Geology **Mathematics** Fitness
Shakespeare **Folklore** Yoga Marketing
Confidence Immortality Biographies
Poetry **Psychology** Witchcraft
Electronics Chemistry History **Law**
Accounting **Philosophy** Anthropology
Alchemy Drama Quantum Mechanics
Atheism Sexual Health **Ancient History**
Entrepreneurship Languages Sport
Paleontology Needlework Islam
Metaphysics Investment Archaeology
Parenting Statistics Criminology
Motivational

Puritan Discipline Tracts.

AN EPISTLE

TO

THE TERRIBLE PRIESTS

OF THE

CONVOCATION HOUSE:

BY

MARTIN MAR-PRELATE, GENTLEMAN.

Re-printed from the Black Letter Edition,

WITH

AN INTRODUCTION AND NOTES.

LONDON:
JOHN PETHERAM, 71, CHANCERY LANE.
1842.

ISBN 978-1-331-86103-4
PIBN 10243427

This book is a reproduction of an important historical work. Forgotten Books uses state-of-the-art technology to digitally reconstruct the work, preserving the original format whilst repairing imperfections present in the aged copy. In rare cases, an imperfection in the original, such as a blemish or missing page, may be replicated in our edition. We do, however, repair the vast majority of imperfections successfully; any imperfections that remain are intentionally left to preserve the state of such historical works.

Forgotten Books is a registered trademark of FB &c Ltd.
Copyright © 2018 FB &c Ltd.
FB &c Ltd, Dalton House, 60 Windsor Avenue, London, SW19 2RR.
Company number 08720141. Registered in England and Wales.

For support please visit www.forgottenbooks.com

INTRODUCTION

The original, from which the following tract is reprinted, is a small quarto volume, in black letter, of 52 pages. There are several tracts which bear the general title of Martin Mar-Prelate, Martin Senior, Martin Junior, &c., but this, which is the "Epistle," and another, called the "Epitome," are frequently confounded together, arising probably from the similarity of appearance in the titles, the first paragraph in each being exactly alike, and the second very similar, though in other respects they differ; and, whereas the "Epistle" was printed "oversea," the "Epitome" (which is a continuation of the Epistle) was "Printed on the other hand of some of the Priests," both without date, though it must have been towards the end of 1588, which may be collected from several circumstances mentioned in the tracts themselves; and, from the appearance of the type, they were most probably printed by Richard Schilders, at Middleburgh, in Zealand. Another reason, perhaps, why these two tracts are so frequently confounded together, may arise from both having been written against the same work, namely, "Dr. John Bridges' Defence of the Government of the Church of England for Ecclesiastical Matters against a Treatise of Ecclesiastical Government," &c., a quarto of 1500 pages, the bulk of which, in more than one instance, appears to have excited Martin's spleen.

The authors of Martin Mar-Prelate were never discovered; it is, however, probable that John Penry, "the hot-headed Welshman," as his enemies called him, was the author. He confessedly wrote several works on behalf of the Puritan cause, and in 1593 suffered death for them.

In the following tract the reader will have an opportunity of judging of the manner in which the other works, announced in the Prospectus, (should sufficient encouragement be given to continue them,) will be published. In the text I have faithfully adhered to the original copy, both in orthography and punctuation; in the notes to the giving some few particulars for illustrating the allusions in the text. Although some of the words to be met with are now obsolete, the readers, into whose hands it will come, will hardly require a glossary of them. The same care in the text, and, I trust, even more attention in the notes, will be given to the subsequent publications.

In conclusion, I must disclaim any personal or politico-religious feelings in bringing once more before the world these curious productions of by-gone times. Personality and scurrility were used freely by the Martinists and their opponents; and however much it is to be wished that they had written with a gravity and decorum more suited to the object they had in view, I could only give that which I found, faithfully and unreservedly, and this I have done.

J. P.

London, Sept. 20th, 1842.

Oh read ouer D. Iohn Bridges, for it is a worthy worke:

Or an epitome of the
fyrste Booke of that right worshipfull vo-
lume, written against the Puritanes, in the defence
of the noble cleargie, by as worshipfull a prieste, Iohn
Bridges, Presbyter, Priest or elder, doctor of Diuillitie,
and Deane of Sarum. Wherein the arguments
of the puritans are wisely prevented, that
when they come to answere M. Doctor,
they must needes say something
that hath bene spoken.

Compiled for the behoofe and overthrow
of the Parsons, Fyckers, and Currats, that have lernt
their Catechismes, and are past grace: By the
reverend and worthie Martin Marprelate
gentleman, and dedicated to the
Confocationhouse.

The Epitome is not yet published, but it shall
be when the Bishops are at conuenient leysure to
view the same. In the meane time, let them
be content with this learned Epistle.

Printed oversea, in Europe, within two fur-
longs of a Bounsing Priest, at the cost and
charges of M. Marprelate, gentleman.

TO THE

RIGHT PUISANTE, AND TERRIBLE PRIESTS,

MY CLEARGIE MASTERS OF THE CONFOCATION-HOUSE,
WHETHER FICKERS GENERALL, WORSHIPFULL PALTRIPOLITANE,
OR ANY OTHER OF THE HOLY LEAGUE OF SUBSCRIPTION:
THIS WORKE I RECOMMEND VNTO THEM WITH ALL MY HEART, WITH
A DESIRE TO SEE THEM ALL SO PROUIDED FOR ONE DAY,
AS I WOULD WISH, WHICH I PROMISE THEM
SHALL NOT BE AT ALL TO THEIR HURT.

RIGHT poysond, persecuting and terrible priests, the theame of mine Epistle, vnto your venerable masterdomes, is of two parts (and the Epitome of our brother Bridges his booke, shall come out speedily). First, most pitifully complayning, Martin Marprelate, &c. Secondly, may it please your good worships, &c.

Most pitifully complayning therefore, you are to vnderstand, that D. Bridges hath written in your defence, a most senceles book, and I cannot very often at one breath come to a full point, when I read the same.

Againe, may it please you to giue me leaue to play the Duns for the nonce as well as he, otherwise dealing with master doctors booke, I cannot keepe *decorum personæ*. And may it please you, if I be too absurd in any place (either in this Epistle, or that Epitome) to ride to Sarum, and thanke his Deanship for it. Because I could not deal with his booke commendablie according to order, vnles I should be sometimes tediously dunstical and absurd. For I haue heard som cleargie men say, that M. Bridges was a verie patch and a duns, when he was in Cambridg. And some say, sauing your reuerence that are Bb. that he is as very a knaue, and enemy vnto the sinceritie of religion, as any popish prelate in Rome. But the patche can doe the cause of sinceritie no hurt. Naye, he hath in this booke wonderfully graced the same by writing against it. For I haue hard some say, that whosoeuer will read his booke, shall as euidently see the goodnes of the cause of reformation, and the poore poore, poore nakednes of your gouernment, as almost in reading all master Cartwright's workes. This was a very great ouersight in his grace of Cant. to suffer such a booke to come out. For besides that an Archb. is very weakely defended by masse Deane, he hath also by this meanes prouoked many to write against his gracious fatherhood, who perhaps neuer ment to take pen in hand. And brother Bridges, mark what Martin tels you, you will shortly I hope haue twenty fistes about your eares more thē your own. Take heed of writing against Puritanes while you liue, yet they say that his grace woulde not haue the booke to be published, and if you marke, you you shall not finde seene and allowed in the title of the booke. Well fare old mother experience yet, the burnt childe dreads the fire: his grace will cary to his graue I warrant you, the blowes which M. Cartwright gaue him in this cause: and therefore no maruell though he was loth to haue any other so banged as he himselfe was to his woe. Others say that Iohn Cant. ouersawe euery proofe. If he did, then he ouersaw many a foule salecisme, many a senceles period, and far more slanders. Slanders my friends? I thinke so. For what will you say, if our brother Bridges, and our cosen Cosins, with manye others, haue had their grace of the Bb. *ad practicandum* in Flanders? Howe could their gouernment stand, vnles they should slander their brethren, and make her Maiestie beleeue, that the Church gouernment prescribed in the worde, would ouerthrow her regiment, if it were receiued in our Church, and that the seekers of reformation, are a sort of Malcontents, and enemies vnto the state.

Item may it please your worthy worshipps, to receive this curteously to favour at my hand, without choller or laughing. For my L. of Winchester is very chollericke and peeuish, so are his betters at Lambeth, and D. Cosins hath a very good grace in iesting, and I woulde he had a little more grace, and a handful or two more of learning, against he answer the Abstract next. Nay beleeue me, it is inough for him to answere the Counterpoyson. And I am none of the malicious sectaries, wherof Iohn of London spake the last Lent, 1588. in his letters written to the Archdeacon of Essex, to forbid publike fastes. Ha, ha, D. Copcot are ye there, why do not you answere the confutation of your sermõ at Pauls crosse? It is a shame for your grace Iohn of Cant. that Cartwrights bookes haue bene now a dozen yeares almost vnanswered: you first prouoked him to write, and you first haue receiued the foyle. If you can answer those books, why do you suffer the Puritans to insult and reioyce at your silence. If you cannot, why are you an Archb. He hath prooued the calling to be vnlawfull and Antichristian. You dare not stand to the defence of it. Now most pitifully complayneth, M. Marprelate, desireth you either to aunswere what hathe beene written against the gracelesnes of your Archbishoprick, or to giue ouer the same, and to be a meanes that no byshop in the land, be a Lord any more. I hope one day her Maiestie will either see that the L. Bb. prooue their calling lawfull by the word, or as Iohn of London prophesied saying, come downe you bishopps from your thousands, and content you with your hundreds, let your diet be pristlike and not princelik, &c. quoth Iohn Elmar in his Harborow of faithful subiects. But I pray you B. Iohn dissolue this one question to your brother Martin: if this prophesie of yours come to passe in your dayes, who shàl be B. of London? And will you not sweare as commonly you do, like a lewd swag, and say, by my faith, by my faith my masters, this geare goeth hard with us. Nowe may it please your grace with ye rest of your worships, to procure that the Puritans may one day haue a free disputatiõ with you, about ye cõtrouersies of the Church, and if you be not set at a flat *non plus*, and quite ouerthrowen, ile be a Lord B. my selfe : looke to your selues, I thinke you haue not long to raigne. Amen. And take heed brethren of your reuerend and learned brother, Martin Marprelate. For he meaneth in these reasons following I can tell you, to proue that you ought not to be maintained by the authoritie of the Magistrate, in any Christian commonwealth : Martin is

a shrewd fellow, and reasoneth thus. Those that are pettie popes and pettie Antichrists, ought not to be maintained in anie Christian commonwealth. But euerie Lord B. in England, as for ilsample, Iohn of Cant. Iohn of London, Iohn Excetor, Iohn Rochester, Thomas of Winchester. The B. of Lincolne, of Worcester, of Peterborow, and to be briefe, all the Bb. in England, Wales, and Ireland, are pettie popes, and pettie Antichristes. Therefore no Lord B. (nowe I pray thee good Martin speake out, if euer thou diddest speake out, that hir Maiestie and the counsell may heare thee) is to be tollerated in any christian common welth : and therefore neither Iohn of Cant. Iohn of London, &c. are to be tollerated in any christian commonwelth. *What malapert knaues are these that cannot be content to stand by and here.but they must teach a gentleman how to speake.*
What say you now brother Bridges is it good writing against Puritanes. Can you denie any part of your learned brother Martin his syllogisme. We denie your minor M. Marprelat say the Bb. and their associats. Yea my learned masters, are you good at that? what do you brethren? say me that againe? do you denie my minor? And *Looke the doctors booke, pag. 107. line 20. and pag.113. line 13.* that be all you can say, to denie L. Bb. to be pettie popes, turne me loose to the priests in y^t point, for I am olde suersvie at the proofe of such matters, ile presently marre the fashion of their Lorships.

They are pettie popes, and pettie Antichrists, whosoeuer vsurpe the authority of pastors ouer them, who by the ordinance of God, are to bee vuder no pastors. For none but Antichristian popes and popelings euer claimed this authoritie vnto themselues, especiallie when it was gainsaid, and accounted Antichristian, generally by the most Churches in the world. But our L. bishops vsurpe authoritie ouer those, who by the ordinance of God, are to be vnder no pastors, and that in such an age, as wherein this authoritie is gainsaid, and accounted Antichristian, generally by all the Churches in the world for ye most part. Therefore our L. Bb. what sayest thou man, our L. bishopps, (I say) as Iohn of Canterburie, Thomas of Winchester (I will spare Iohn of London for this time, for it may be he is at boules, and it is pitie to trouble my good brother, lest he should sweare too bad) my reuerend prelate of Litchfielde, with the rest of that swinishe rable, are pettie Antichrists, pettie popes, proud prelates, intollerable withstanders of reformation, enemies of the gospell, and most couetous wretched priests.

M. Marprelate you put more than the question in the conclusion of your syllogisme.

This is a pretie matter, y^t standers by, must be so busie in other mens games: why sawceboxes must you be pratling? you are as mannerly as bishops, in medling with that you haue nothing to doe, as they do in taking vpon them ciuill offices. I thinke for any maners either they or you haue, that you were brought up in Bridewell. But it is well that since you last interrupted me (for now this is the second time) you seeme to haue lernt your *Cato de moribus* in that you keepe your selues on the margent. Woulde you be answered? Then you must know, that I haue set downe nothing but the trueth in the conclusion, and the syllogismes are mine owne,

I may do what I will with them, and thus holde you content. But what say you my horned masters of the Confocation house? you denie my minor againe I know. And thus I prooue it. First

That our Prelates vsurpe their authoritie.

They vsurpe their authoritie, who violently and vnlawfully, retaine those vnder their gouernment, that both woulde and ought (if they might) to shake of that yoke wherewith they are kept vnder. But our Lord bishops retaine such (namely other pastors) and vnlawfully vnder their yoke, who both woulde and ought to reiect the same. For all the pastors in the land, that deserue the names of pastors, are against their wil vnder the bishops iurisdictions. And they are vnlawfully detained by them, because no pastor can be lawfully kept vnder the pastoral (I meane not the ciuill) authoritie of any one man. Therfore our Bb. and proud popish, presumptuous, profane, paultrie, pestilent and pernicious prelates, bishop of Hereforde and all: are first vsurpers to beginne the matter withall. Secondly

Our Prelates claime this authoritie ouer those, who by the ordinance of God, are to be vnder no Pastors.

That is, they claime pastorall authoritie ouer other ministers and pastors, who by the ordinaunce of God, are appointed to be pastors and shepheards to feede others, and not sheep, or such as are to haue shepheards, by whõ they are to be fedd and ouerseene: whiche authoritie the bishops claime vnto themselues. For they say that they are pastors of al the pastors within their dioces. And take this of M. Marprelates worde, that there is no pastor of pastors, but he is a pope. For who but a pope will claime this authoritie. Thirdly,

This authoritie of our L. Bb. in England, is accounted Antichristian of the most Churches in the worlde.

As of the Heluetian, the Scottish, French, Bohemian, and the Churches of the low countries, the Churches of Polonia, Denmarke, within the dominions of the Count Palatine, of the Churches in Saxonie, and Sweuia, &c. which you shall see euidently proued in the Harmonie of the Confessions of all those Churches, Section the eleuenth. Which Harmonie, was translated and printed by that puritan Cambridg printer, Thomas Thomas. And although the booke came out by publike authoritie, yet by your leaue the Bishops haue called them in, as things against their state. And trust me, his grace will owe that puritane printer as good a turne, as hee paide vnto Robert Walde-graue for his sawciness in printing my frend and deare brother Diotrephes his Dialogue. Well frend Thomas I warne you before hand, looke to your selfe.

And now brethren byshops, if you wil not beleeue me, I wil set down the very words of the French confession, contayned page 359. of the Harmonie. We beleeue (saith the confession, art 30.) that all true pastors, in what place soeuer they be placed, haue the same, and equall authority among thēselues, giuen vnto them vnder Iesus Christ the onely head, and the chiefe alone vniuersal bishop: and that therefore it is not lawfull for anye Churche to challenge vuto it selfe, dominion or soueraignty ouer any other. What an horrible heresie is this, wil some say, why? gentle Martin, is it possible y' these words of the French confession should be true? is it possible that there ought to be an equallity betweene his Grace and the Deane of Sarum, or som other hedge priest: Martin saith it ought be so, why then Martin if it shoulde be so, howe will the byshops satisfie the reader in this poynt? Alas simple fellow whatsoeuer thou art, I perceiue thou dost not mark the words of the confession: My good brethren haue long since taken order for this geare: For the Confession doth not say that all Pastors, but that all true Pastors, and all Pastors that are vnder Iesus Christ, are of equall authority. So that all men see that my brethren, which are neyther true Pastors, nor I feare me vnder Jesus Christ, ar not to be of equall authority. And because this doth not touch them, I will end this whole learned discourse with the words of Pope Gregorie, vuto Iohn bishop of Constantinople (for I haue red somthing in my dayes) which words you shall finde in our owne Englishe Confession, written by a bish. page 361. of the Harmony. The Popes words be these, "He is also the king of pride, he is Lucifer, which preferreth himself before his brethren, he hath forsaken the fayth, and is the forerunner of Antichriste." And haue not I quited my selfe like a man, and dealt very valiantly, in prouing that my lerned brethren the L. bishops ought not to be in any christian

At a dead lift well fare a good glose.

Put the case that my Lord of Canterbury is such a one.

common wealth, because they are pettie Popes, and pettie Antichristes. But what doe you say, if by this lustie syllogisme of mine owne making, I proue thē Popes once more for recreations sake.

Whosoeuer therefore clayme vnto themselues pastorall authoritie ouer those Christians, with whome they cannot possiblie at any time altogether in the same congregation sanctifie the Sabboth : they are vsurping prelats, Popes and pettie Antichrists : For did you euer here of anye but of Popes and dumb ministers, that woulde challenge the authority of Pastors ouer those Christians, vnto whom they could not possiblie on the Sabboths discharge the dutie of pastors : But our L. Bb. challenge vnto themselues pastorall authoritie ouer them, vnto whom they cannot possiblie on the Sabboth, discharge the duty of Pastors, vz. ouer people inhabiting diuers shires distant asunder, with whom, gathered together on the Sabboth, they cannot by order of nature, performe any dutie of Pastors : Therefore all the L. Bishops in England, Ireland and Wales (and for the good wil I beare to the reuerende brethren, I will speake as loud as euer I can) All our L. Bb. I saye, are pettie Popes, and pettie vsurping Antichristes, and I thinke if they will still continue to be so, that they will breed yong Popes and Antichristes: *per consequens*, neyther they nor theyr broode, are to be tollerated in any Christian common wealth, quoth Martin Marprelate. There is my judgment of you brethren, make y[e] most of it, I hope it will neuer

Why Martin, what meanest thou? Certainely an thou takest that course but a while, thou wilt set thy good brethren at their wits end.

be worth a byshopricke vnto you: reply when you dare, you shall haue as good as you bring. And if you durst but dispute with my worship in these poynts, I doubt not but you should be sent home by weeping crosse. I wold wish you my venerable masters for all that, to answere my resons, or out of doubt you will prooue pettie Antichristes, Your corner caps and tippets will do nothing in this poynt.

Most pitifully complayneth, Martin Marprelate, vnto your honorable masterships, that certayn theeues, hauing stolne from dyars in Thames streat, as much cloth as came to 30. pound, did hide the sayd cloth in Fulham, which is a place within the territories of the Lord dumbe Iohn, who by occupation is Lord Bish. of London: The theeues were apprehended, the cloth came within your clouches Don Iohn of London, and al is fish that comes to the net with your good honor. The theeues being taken, the dyars came to challenge their cloth: Iohn London the bishop, said it was his owne, because it was taken within his owne Lordship. But sayth he, if the cloth be yours, let the law go vpon the theeues, and then ile talke farther with you: wel, one or two of the theeues were executed, and at their deathes confessed that to be the cloth which the bishop had, but the dyars coulde not get their cloth, nor cannot vnto this day, no though one of their honors wrote vnto him to restore the cloth vnto the poore men. What reason were it he should giue thē their own, as though he could not tell how to put it vnto good vses as well as the right owners. It is very good blew, and so would serue well for the liueries of his men, and it was good greene, fit to make quishions and couerings for tables. Brother London, you were best to make restitution, it is playne theft and horrible oppression: Boner would haue blusht, to haue bene taken with the like fact. The popish sort your brethren, will commend this vnto posteritie by writing assure your selfe. The dyars names are Banghin, Swan and Price: They dwell at the old swan in Thames streat, I warrant you Martin will be found no lyar, he bringeth in nothing without testimonie. And therefore I haue set downe the mens names and the places of their aboade, y^t you of this conspiration house may finde out this slaunder of trueth, against the L. of good London. It was not therefore for nothing. (Iohn of London I perceiue) that Mistris Lawson the shrew at Pauls gate, and enemie to all dumb dogs and tyrannicall Prelates in the land: bad you throw downe your selfe at hir Maiesties feet, acknowledging your selfe to be vnsauory salt, and to craue pardon of her highnes, because you had so long deceiued her and her people: You might well ynough craue pardon for your theft, for Martin wil stand to it, that the detayning of the mens cloth is plain theft.

My booke shall come with a witness before the high commission.

Riddle me a riddle what is that, his grace threatened to send Mistris Lawson to Bridewell, because she shewed the good father D. Perne, a way how to get his name out of the booke of Martyrs, where the turnecoat is canonized for burning Bucers bones: Dame Lawson aunswered, that she was an honest Citizens wife, a man well knowen, and therefore bad his Grace an he would, send his uncle Shorie thither. Ha ha ha: Now good your grace you shall haue small gaynes in medling with Margrete Lawson I can tell you. For if she be cited before *Tarquinius Superbus* D. Stanop, she will desire him to deal as fauorablie with her in that cause, as he would with Mistris Blackwell, tse tse tse, wil it neuer be better with you mistris Lawson.

Sohow, brother Bridges, when wil you answere the booke intituled, an answere to Bridges his slanders: nay I thinke you had more need to gather a beneuolence among the Cleargie, to pay Charde toward the printing of your booke, or els labour to his grace to get him another protection, for men wil giue no mony for your book, vnles it be to stop mustard pots, as your brother Cosins answer to the Abstract did. You haue bin a worthy writer as they say of a long time, your first book was a proper Enterlude, called Gammar Gurtons needle. But I thinke that this trifle, which sheweth the author to haue had some witte and inuention in him, was none of your doing: Because your bookes seeme to proceede from the braynes of a woodcocke, as haning neyther wit nor learning. Secondly, you haue to your mediocritie written against the Papists: And since that time, you haue written a sheete in rime, of all the names attributed vnto the Lorde in the Bible, a worthy monument: what hath the hedge priest my brother written anye more? O is, I crye him mercy, he hath written this great volume which now I haue in hand against his brethren. The qualities of this booke are many, M. D.

sheweth himselfe to be very skilfull in the learning of *ob* and *Sol,* if euer you red olde Fa-Briccot vpon Aristotle: M. Deanes manner of writing and his, are not much vnlike, Doctor Terence of Oxforde and this Doctor, may be neere of kindred for their learning. There bee periods in this learned booke of great reason, though altogether without sence. I will giue you a proof or two, page 441. "And although" (sayth the Doctor) "Paul afterward, 1 Cor. 1. 14. mentioning this Crispus, term him not there, the archgouer- nour of the Iewes Synagogue, yet as it farther appeareth, Acts 18. 17. by Sosthenes, who was long before a faythfull Christian, and as some alledge out of Eusebius lib. 1. cap. 13. he was also one of the 72. Disciples chosen by Christ."

<small>Sosthenes, and not Crispus was one of the 72. Disciples.</small>

Fleering, ieering, leering: there is at all no sence in this period. For the words (yet afterward) vnto the ende, M. D. minde was so set vpon a byshopricke, that he brought nothing concerning Crispus to aunswere the word (yet) Therefore I will helpe my reuerende brother to make the sentence in this sort. And although, &c. yet afterwarde my learned brother, D. Yong, Bish. of Rochester, hauing the presentation of a benefice in his hand, presented himselfe thereunto, euen of meere good-wil. I Iohn of Rochester, present Iohn Young quoth the bishop. Nowe iudge you good readers, whether Martin sayth not true, that there is too much cousenage now a dayes among the cleargie men.

This sentence following of M. Deanes, hath as good sence as the former, page 655. The D. citeth these wordes out of the learned Discourse. " God graunt that in steede of ordinarye formes of prayers, wee may haue preaching in all places." And in steede of Amen, God forbidd saye I, quoth the Doctor, with another prayer to the contrarye, (nowe marke my masters, whether you can finde anye sence in this contrarye prayer, for I assure you reuerende Martin can find none) " if it be his good will not so much (good lord) to pun- nish vs, that this our brethrens prayer should be graunted." If this be a senceles kind of writing, I would there were neuer a Lord bishop in England. *These be the D. owne words.*

And lerned brother Bridges, a man might almost run himselfe out of breath before he could come to a full point in many places in your booke, page 69. line 3. speaking of the extraordinarye giftes in the Apostles time, you haue this sweete learning. " Yea some of them haue for a great part of the time, continued euen till our times, and yet continue, as the operation of great workes, or if they meane miracles, which were not ordinary no not in that extraordinary time, and as the hipocrites had them, so might and had diuers of the papists, and yet their cause neuer the better, and the like may we say of the gift of speking with tongs, which haue not bin with studie before learned, as Anthonie, &c. and diners also among the ancient fathers, and some among the papists, *who who! Dean take breath and then to it againe.* and some among vs, haue not bene destitute of the giftes of prophesying, and much more may I saye this of the gift of healing, for none of those giftes or graces giuen then or since, or yet to men infer the grace of Gods election to be of necessitie to saluation."

Here is a good matter deliuered in as good Gramaticall words: But what say you if M. Do. can prooue that Peter was prince of the Apostles? That is popery (quoth Martin) to begin withal. Nay but what say you if he proueth that one priest among the residue, may haue a lawfull superiour authoritie ouer the vniuersall bodye of the Church, is not this plaine treason? Is forsooth, if a puritane had written it: But Mas Deane of Sarum that wrote these things, is a man that fauoreth bishops, a nonresident, one that will not sticke to play a game at Cards, and sweare by his trothe: and therefore he may write against the puritans what he will, his grace of Canterbury will giue a verye Catholike exposition thereof. This geare maynteineth the crowne of Canterbury, and what matter is it though hee write for the maintenaunce thereof, all the treason in the world. It wil neuer come vnto hir Maiesties eare, as my friend Tertullus in the poore Dialogue that the bishops lately burned hath set downe. His grace is able to salue the matter well inough: yea my brother Bridges himselfe can aunswere this poynt. For hee hath written otherwise, page 288. line 26. in these wordes: " Neither is all gouernment taken away from all, though a moderate superior gouernment be giuen of all to some, and not yet of all in all the Churche to one, but to one ouer some in seuerall and particular Churches." The Deane wil say, that concerning the superioritie of bishops this

Both these poynts are set down page 448. line 3.

is the meaning. As concerning the treason, written page 448. it may be the foxe D. Perne, who helped him as they say, to make this worthy volume, was the author of it.

Now brethren, if any of you that are of the Confocation house, would knowe howe I can prooue M. Deane to haue written flatt treason, page 448. as I haue before set downe: draw neere, and with your patience I will proue it so, that M. Deane will stand to his owne words, which I care not if they be sett downe: page 448. line 3. Thus you shall read, " Doth S. Peter then forbid that any one Elder should haue and exercise any superior gouernment ouer the cleargie," vnderstanding the cleargie in this sence, " if he doth not but alloweth it, and his selfe practized it: thē howsoeuer both the name, both of gouerning and cleargy may be abused, the matter is cleare, that one priest or elder among the residue, may haue a superior authority ouer the cleargie, that is, ouer all the vniuersall bodie of the church, in euery particular or seuerall congregation, and so not only ouer the people, but also ouer the whol order of ministers." *I commend thee yet good D. for thy good English tongue.* *Cleare quoth he, yea who will make any question thereof.*

Would your worships knowe howe I can shew and conuince my brother Bridges, to haue set downe flat treason in the former words, Then haue at you Deane. 1. It is treason to affirme her Maiestie to be an infidell or not to be contayned in the bodie of the Church. 2. It is treason to saye that one priest or elder, may haue a lawfull superiour *Looke Stat. 13. Elizabeth.*

authoritie ouer hir Maiestie. Take your spectacles
then, and spell your owne words, and you shall finde
that you haue affirmed eyther of these 2. poynts. For
you affirme that a priest may haue a lawfull superior
authoritie ouer the vniuersall bodie of the Churche.
And you dare not denie her Maiestie to bee contayned
within the vniversall bodie of the Church. Therefore
to helpe you to spell your conclusion, you haue written
treason, if you will be as good as your writing: your
learned frend Martin (for no brother M. Deane if you
be a traytor) would not mistake you, and therefore say
what you can for your selfe: you meane not that this
priest shalbe ouer all the church: do you? but howe
shall we knowe that? forsooth because you saye that
this superioritie must be in euery particular or seuerall
congregation. Is this your aunswere brother Iohn?
why what sence is there in these words? One priest
may haue a superior authoritie ouer the vniuersall body
of the Church, in euery particular or seuerall congregation? The vniuersal bodie of the Church, is now become a particular or seuerall congregation with you?
And in good earnest Deane Iohn, tell me howe many
orders of ministers be there in a particular cōgregation?
For there must bee orders of ministers in the congregation, where you meane this bounsing priest should
haue his superioritie, and because this cannot be in
seuerall and particular congregations: therefore you cannot meane by these words, ouer the vniuersall bodye of
the Church, any other thing, then the whole Church
militant: But you would mende your answere? And

say that this superior priest must be an Englishe priest
and no forrainer: As for ilsample, his grace A good il-
of Canterbury is an English priest.   Do you sample.
meane then, that his grace should be this superior priest,
who by Sir Peters allowaunce may haue a Sir Peter
lawfull superior authoritie ouer the vniuersall neuer alow-
bodie of the Churche?   Truely I doe not ed this.
meane so.   And good now, do not abuse his graces
worship in this sort, by making him a Pope.   Be it
you meane this hie priest should be no stranger, yet
your treason is as great or greater.   For you will haue
her Maiesty to be subiect vnto her owne subiect and
seruant.   And if it be treason to say that the Pope, who
hath princes and Cardinalls for his seruants, being far
better than were Iohn with his Canterburinesse, may
haue a lawfull superior authoritie ouer her Maiesty, as
one being contained with in the vniuersall bodie of the
Church: is it not much more trayterous to say, that an
Englishe vassall may haue this authoritie ouer his
Soueraigne.   And brother Iohn, did Sir Peter his selfe
in deede practize this authoritie?   whie what Here be
a priest was he?   Did he alow others to haue those that
                                                can be bar-
this authority.   Truly this is more then euer I barous as
                                                well as
knew til now.   Yet notwithstanding, I thinke masse
                                                Deane.
he neuer wore corner cap and tippet in all his
life, nor yet euer subscribed to my Lord of Canterbury
his articles: Now the question is, whom Sir Peter his
selfe nowe alloweth to be this bouncing priest? the Pope
of Rome yea or no?   No in no case, for that is against
the statute.   For will my brother Bridges saye that the

Pope may haue a lawfull superior authoritie ouer his Grace of Canterbury? Ile neuer beleeue him though he saye so. Neyther will I saye that his Grace is an Infidell, (nor yet sweare that he is much bet- ter) and therefore M. Deane meaneth not that the Pope shoulde bee this highe Priest. No brother Martin (quoth M. Deane) you saye true, I meane not that the Pope is this priest of Sir Peter. And I haue many reasons why I shoulde denie him this authoritie. First he is a massemonger, that is, a professed idolater. 2. He weareth a triple crowne, so doth not my Lorde of Canterbury. 3. He hath his seat in Romish Babylon in Rome within Italie: you know ye nomber 666. in the Reuelation signifieth *La-tenios*, that is, the man of Rome, or *Ecclesia Italike*, the Italian church. Lastly, he must haue men to kisse his toes, and must be carried vpon mens shulders, and must haue princes and kings to attend vpon him, which shew-eth his horrible pride. Sir Peters vniuersall priest and mine, shalbe no such priest I trow, ka Mas Doctor. No shall not Doctor Iohn, I con thee thank. Then thy vniuersall priest, 1. must be no idolator, 2. must be no proude priest, and haue neuer a triple crowne (and yet I hope he may weare as braue a sattin gowne as my Lord of Winchester weareth, and be as cholericke as he) 3. he must haue his seat out of Italie, as for fashion sake, at *Lambehith Hippo*, &c. but at Rome in no case. If I should examine these properties, I thinke some of them, if not all, haue bene accidents vnto English priests. For how many Bb. are there in England, which haue

<small>His grace shall neuer get me to sweare against my conscience.</small>

not either said masse, or helped the priest to say masse or bene present at it? As for the triple crowne, Pope Ioan the English harlot hath woon it: So did Vrbane the 5. an English man. And concerning pride, I hope that our Bb. nowe liuing, haue to their mediocritie taken order, that some Popes may be inferior vnto them, as for ilsample, his Canterburinesse, &c. And I cannot see how the planting of the chaire in Rome anye more then Canterbury, can make a Pope. Seeing that Clement the 5. Iohn 22. Benedict 12. and all other Popes, from the yeare 1306. vnto 1375. sate not in Rome, but for the most part at Avinion in Fraunce. But notwithstanding all this, out of your meaning masse D. such a simple ingram man as I am, in these poynts, of vniuersall superior priests, I finde three differences betweene my L. of Peterborough, or any other our high priests in England, and the Popes holines: and 3. impediments to hinder the Pope from being Sir Peters high priest and yours, vz. his idolatrie, 2. his triple crowne, 3. his seat at Rome. But if Hildebrande Pope of Rome, had beene a professor of the trueth (as his grace Doctor turnecoats (Perne I shoulde saye) scholler is) had worne no triple crowne, had bene Archbishop of Canterbury (and I think we haue had Hildebrands there ere nowe) then he might by the iudgement of the learned Bridges, and the allowance of that Peter, which his selfe practized that authoritie, haue a lawful superior authority ouer the vniuersal bodie of the Church. And what a worthy Canterbury Pope had this bin, to be called my Lords grease? Thus you see Brother Bridges,

M. Marprelate an please him, is able to make a yonger brother of you: he hath before proued, that if euer you be Archb. of Canterbury (for you wrote this foule heape against the holy Discipline of Christ, (as Whitgift did the like) in hope to bee the next Pope of Lambeth) that then you shalbe a pettie Pope, and a pettie Antichrist: Nay he hath prooued you to haue deserued a cawdell of Hempseed, and a playster of neckweed, as weel as some of your brethren the papists. And now brother Bridges once again, is it good writing against the Puritans. Take me at my word, vnlesse you answere the former poynt of Antichristianisme, and this of treason, I will neuer write again to my bre[thren] the Bb. but as to vsurpers and Antichristes, and I shall take you for no better then an enemie to her Maiesties Supremacie. And because you haue taken vppon you to defend L. Bb. though you be as very a sot as euer liued, (outcept dumb Iohn of London againe) yet you shall answere my reasons, or else I will so course you, as you were neuer coursed since you were a Symonical Deane, you shall not deale with my worshipp, as Iohn with his Canterburinesse did with Thomas Cartwright, whiche Iohn, left the cause you defend in the plaine field, and for shame threw downe his weapons with a desperate purpose to runne away, and leaue the cause, as he like a coward hath done: For this dozen yeares we neuer saw any thing of his in printe for the defence of his cause, and poore M. Cartwright doth content himselfe with the victorie, which the other will not (though in deed he hath by his silence) seeme to grant. But

I will not be this vsed at your hands, for vnlesse you answere me, or confesse (and that in print) that all L. Bb. in England, Wales, Ireland, yea and Scotlande to, are pettie popes, and plaine vsurpers, and pettie Antichristes: Ile kindle such a fire in the holes of these foxes, as shall neuer be quenched as long as there is a L. B. in England. *Ha, prieste ile bang you, or else neuer trust me.* And who but the worthie Martin can doe so valiantly. Page 560. master Deane bringeth in Aretius, to proue that kneeling at the communion is not offensiue. And how is the argument concluded think you? for sooth euen thus. Aretius saith, that in Berne they receiue the communiō sitting or standing: therefore saith my brother Bridges, kneeling at the communion is not vnlawfull. I maruell whether he was not hatched in a goose nest, that would thus conclude.

In another place, page 226. or thereabouts, he prooueth that one man may haue two spirituall linings, because the puritans themselues saye, that one charge may haue two ministers, to wit, a Pastor and a Doctor. And these be some of the good profes whereby our established gouernment is vphelde. *My brother Bridges nowe reasoneth in good earnest for nonresidents.*

It would make a man laugh, to see how many trickes the Doctor hath to coosen the sielie puritans in his book, he can now and then without any noyse, alleadge an author clean against himselfe, and I warrant you, wipe his mouth cleanly, and looke another way, as though it had not bene he. I haue laught as though I had bene tickled, to see with *What a craftie knaue is masse Deane.*

what sleight he can throw in a popish reason, and who sawe him? And with what art, he can conuaye himselfe from the question, and goe to another matter? it is wonderfull to thinke. But what would not a Deane do to get a bishoppricke? In this one poynt, for sparing labour he is to bee admired, that he hath set downe vnder his owne name, those things which (to speake as I think) he neuer wrote himselfe. So let the puritans aunswere when they will, he hath so much of other mens helpes, and such contrarieties in this book, that when they bring one thing against him out of his owne writings, he wil bring another place out of the sayd booke, flat contrary to that, and say that the latter is his, and not the former. For the former, it may bee, was some other friends, not so fullie seen in the cause, as presbyter Iohn Bridges was. The reason of these contrarieties was uery expedient: because many had a hand in the worke, euery man wrote his own minde, and masse doctor ioyned the whole together.

Nowe forasmuch as he hath playd the worthy workeman, I will bestow an Epitaph vpon his graue when he dyeth, which is thus:

"Here lies Iohn Bridges, a worthie Presbyter he was."

But what if he be a B. before he die? what brethren? doe you not thinke that I haue two strings to my bow, is vs haue I, and thus I sing, if he chance to be a bishop.

"Here lies Iohn Bridges late Bishop, friend to the Papa."

OF THE CONFOCATION HOUSE. 25

I care not an I now leaue masse Deanes worship, and be eloquent once in my dayes: yet brother Bridges, a worde or two more with you, ere we depart, I praye you where may a mā buie such another gelding, and borow such another hundred poundes, as you bestowed vpon your good patron Sir Edward Horsey, for his good worde in helping you to your Deanry: go to, go to, I perceiue you will prooue a goose. Deale closeliar for shame the next time: must I needs come to the knoledge of these things? What if I should report abroad, that cleargie men come vnto their promotions by Simonie? haue not you giuen me iuste cause? I thinke Simonie be the bishops lacky. Tarleton tooke him not long since in Don Iohn of Londons cellor.

Well nowe to mine eloquence, for I can doe it I tell you. Who made the porter of his gate a dumb minister? Dumbe Iohn of London. Who abuseth her Maiesties subiects, in vrging them to subscribe contrary to lawe? Iohn of London. Who abuseth the high commission, as much as any? Iohn London, (and D. Stanop to) Whoe bound an Essex minister, in 200.l. to weare the surplice on Easter day last? Iohn London. Who hath cut downe the Elmes at Fulham? Iohn London. Who is a carnall defender of the breache of the Sabboth in all the places of his abode? Iohn London. *Ile make you weary of it dumbe John, except you leaue persecuting.* Who forbiddeth men to humble themselues in fasting and prayer before the Lorde, and then can say vnto the preachers, now you were best to tell the people, that we forbidd fastes? Iohn London. Who goeth to bowles vpon the Sabboth ? Dumbe dunsticall Iohn of good London, hath done all this. I will for this time leaue this figure, and tell your venerable masterdomes a tale worth the hearing: I had it at the second hand: if he that tolde it me, added any thing, I do not commende him, but I forgiue him: The matter is this. A man dying in Fulham, made one of the bishopp of Londons men his executor. The man had bequeathed certaine Legacies vnto a poore shephearde in the towne. The shepheard could get nothing of the bishops man, and therefore made his mone vnto a gentleman of Fulham, that belongeth to the court of requests. The gentlemans name is **M. Madox**. The poore mans case came to bee tryed in the court of Requestes. The B. man desired his masters helpe: Dumb Iohn wrote to the Masters of requests to this effect, and I think these were his wordes.

" My masters of the requests, the bearer hereof being my man, hath a cause before you: in as much as I vnderstande howe the matter standeth, I praye you let my man be discharged the court, and I will see an agreement made. Fare you well." The letter came to M. D. Dale, he answered it in this sort.

" My Lorde of London, this man deliuered your letter, I pray you gine him his dinner on Christmas day for his labour, and fare you well."

Dumbe Iohn not speeding this way, sent for the sayd M. Madox: he came, some rough words passed on both sides, Presbyter Iohn sayde, master Madox was verye sawcie, especially seeing he knew before whom he spake:

namely, the Lord of Fulham. Wherevnto the gentleman answered, that he had bene a pore freeholder in
Fulham, before Don Iohn came to be L. there, hoping
also to be so, when he and all his brood (my Ladle his
daughter and all) shoulde be gone. At the hearing of
this speeche, the waspe got my brother by the nose,
which mad him in his rage to affirme, that he woulde
be L. of Fulham as long as he liued, in despight of all
England. Naye softe there, quoth M. Madox, except
her Maiestie I pray you, that is my meaning, ka dumb
Iohn, and I tell thee Madox, that thou art but a Iacke
to vse me so: master Madoxe replying, sayd that in
deed his name was Iohn, and if euery Iohn were a Iacke,
he was content to bee a Iacke (there he hit my L. ouer
the thumbs) The B. growing in choller, sayd y^t master
Madox his name did shewe what he was, for sayth he,
thy name is mad Oxe, which declareth thee to be an
vnruly and mad beast. M. Madox answered againe,
that the B. name, if it were descanted vpon, did most
significantly shew his qualities. For said he, you are
called Elmar, but you may be better called marelme,
for you haue marred all the Elmes in Fulham: hauing
cut them all downe. This farre is my worthy story, as
worthye to bee printed, as any part of Deane Iohns
booke, I am sure.

Item, may it please you that are L. Bb. to shewe
your brother Martin, how you can escape the danger of
a premunire, seeinge you vrge her Maiesties subiects to
subscribe, cleane contrary to the Statute 13. Elizabeth.
What haue you to shew for your selues, for I tell you,

I heard some say, that for vrging subscription, you were all within the premunire, insomuch that you haue bene drinen closely to buie your pardons, you haue forfayted all that you haue vnto her Maiestie, and your persons are voyde of her Maiesties protection: you knowe the danger of a premunire, I trowe? Well but tell me what you haue to shewe for your selues? her Maiesties prerogatiue? haue you? Then I hope you haue it vnder seale. No I warrant you, her Maiesty is too wise for that. For it shall neuer be sayde, that she euer authorized such vngodly proceedings, to the dishonor of God, and the wounding of the consciences of her best subiects. Seeing you haue nothing to shew that it is her Maiesties will, why should any man subscribe contrary to statute? Forsooth mē must beleue such honest creatures as you are on your words? must they? As though you would not lye: yes, yes, bishops will lye like dogs. They were neuer yet well beaten for their lying.

May it please your honorable worships, to let worthy Martin vnderstand, why your Canterburinesse and the rest of the L. Bb. fauor papists and recusants, rather thē puritans. For if a puritane preacher, hauing a recusant in his parrish, and shall go about to deale with the recusant for not comming to Church. Sir will the recusant say, you and I will answere the matter before his grace, (or other the high commissioners, as L. Bb. Seeuillaines (I meane) popish doctors of the bawdie courts.) And assoone as the matter is made knowne vnto my Lorde, the preacher is sure to go by the worst, and the recusan to carie all the honestie: Yea the preacher shalbe busie enuious fellow, one that doth not obserue the booke, and conforme himself according vuto order, and perhaps go home by beggers bush, for any benefice he hath to line vpon. For it may be the Bb. will be so good vnto him, as to depriue him for not subscribing. As for the recusant, he is known to be a man that must haue the libertie of his conscience. Is this good dealing brethren. And is it good dealing, that poore men should be so troubled to the chauncellors courte, that they are euen wearie of their lines, for such horrible oppression as there raignes. I tell you D. Stannop (for all you are so proude) a premunire will take you by the backe one day, for oppressing and tyrannizing ouer her Maiesties subiects as you doe.

Doth your grace remember, what the Iesuit at Newgate sayde of you, namely, that my Lorde of Canterbury should surely be a Cardinall, if euer poperie did come againe into England: (yea and that a braue Cardinall to) what a knaue was this Iesuit? beleeue me I would not say thus much of my Lord of Canterburie, for a thousand pound, lest a *Scandalum magnatum* should be had against me: But well fare him that sayd thought is free.

Pitifully complayning, is there any reason, (my Lords grace) why knaue Thackwell the printer, which printed popishe and trayterous welshe bookes in Wales, shoulde haue more fauour at your gracelesse bandes, then poore Walde-graue, who neuer printed book against you, that contayneth eyther treason or impietie. Thackwell is at libertie to walke where he will, and permitted to make the most he could of his presse and letters: whereas Robert Walde-graue dares not shew his face for the blood-thirstie desire you haue for his life, onely for printing of bookes which toucheth the bishops Myters. You know that Walde-graues printing presse and Letters were takken away: his presse being timber, was sawen and hewed in pieces, the yron work battered and made vnseruiceable, his Letters melted, with cases and other tooles defaced (by Iohn Woolfe, alias Machiuill, Beadle of the Stacioners, and most tormenting executioner of Walde-graues goods) and he himselfe vtterly depriued for euer printing againe, hauing a wife and sixe small children. Will this monstrous crueltie neuer be reuenged thinke you? When Walde-graues goods was to be spoiled and defaced, there were some printers, that rather then all the goods should be spoyled, offered money for it, towardes the reliefe of the mans wife and children, but this coulde not be obtayned, and yet popishe Thackwell, though hee printed popish and trayterous bookes, may haue the fauor to make money of his presse and letters. And reason to. For Walde-graues profession ouerthroweth the popedome of Lambehith, but Thackwels popery maintayneth the same. And now that Walde-graue hath neither presse nor letters, his grace may dine and sup the quieter. But looke to it brother Canterburie, certainly without your repentance, I feare me, you shalbe * Hildebrand in deed. Walde-graue hath left house and home, by reason of your vnnaturall tyrannie: hauing left behinde him a poore wife and sixe Orphanes, with-

<small>A fyrebrand in deede.</small>

out any thing to relieue them. (For the husband, you haue bereaued both of his trade and goods) Be you assured that the crie of these will one day preuaile against you, vnlesse you desist from persecuting. And good your grace, I do now remember my selfe of another printer, that had presse and letter in a place called Charterhouse in London (in Anno 1587. neere about the time of the Scottish Queenes death) inteligence was giuen vnto your good grace of the same, by some of the Stacioners of London, it was made knowen vnto you what worke was in hand, what letter the booke was on, what volume, vz. in 8o. in halfe sheetes, what workemen wrohgt on the same: namely, I. C. the Earle of Arundels man and three of his seruants, with their seuerall names, what liberallitie was bestowed on those workemen, and by whom, &c. Your grace gaue the Stacioners the hearing of this matter, but to this daye the parties were neuer calde in Coram for it: but yet by your leaue my Lord, vpon this information vnto your honorable worship, the stacioners had newes, that it was made knowne vuto the printers, what was done vnto your good grace, and presently in steed of the work which was in hand, there was other appointed, as they saye, authorized by your Lordship. I will not saye it was your owne doing, but by your sleeue, thought is free. And my good L. (nay you shalbe none of my L. but M. Whitgift and you will) are you partiall or no in all your actions tell me? yes you are? I wil stand to it? did

More knauery.

Is not he a very Pope in deed that thus hideth poperie and knauery.

It may be you hindred her Maiestie of many thousands of pounds.

you get a decree in the high court of Starchamber onely for Walde-graue? if it bee in generall (and you not partiall) why fet you not that printing presse and letters out of Charterhouse, and destroye them as you did Walde-graues? Why did you not apprehend the parties, why? Because it was poperie at the least, that was printed in Charterhouse: and that maintayneth the crowne of Canterburye? And what is more tollerable than popery? Did not your grace of late erecte a new printer contrary to the foresayd decree? One Thomas Orwine (who sometimes wrought popish bookes in corners: namely Iesus Psalter, our Ladies Psalter, &c.) with condition he should print no such seditious bookes as Walde-graue hath done? Why my Lord? Walde-graue neuer printed any thing against the state, but onely against the vsurped state of your Paultripolitanship, and your pope holy brethren, the Lorde B. and your Antichristian swinish rable, being intollerable withstanders of reformation, enemies of the Gospell, and most couetous wretched, and popish priests.

<small>This is no knauery my Lord.</small>

Nowe most pitifully complayning, Martin Marprelate: That the papistes will needs make vs beleeue, that our good Iohn of Canterbury and they, are at no great iarre in religion. For Reignolds the papist at Rheimes, in his booke against M. Whitakers, cōmendeth the works written by his grace, for the defence of the corruption in our Churche, against T. Cartwright. And sayth that the said Iohn Cant. hath many things in him, which euidently shew a catholike perswasion. Alas my masters shall we loose our metropolitan in this sort. Yet the note is a good note, that we may take heed the Spaniards steale him not away, it were not amisse if her Maiestie knew of it. Wee need not fear (if we can keep him) the Spaniards and our other popish enemies, because our metropolitans religion and theirs differ not much. In the article of Christes descending into hell, they iumpe in one right pat: and in the mayntenaunce of the hierarchie of Bb. and ascribing the name of priest, vnto them that are ministers of the gospel. I know not whether my next tale will be acceptable vnto his grace or not. But haue it among you my masters : M. Wiggington the pastor of Sidborough, is a man not altogether unknowen vnto you. And I think his worshipfull grace got little or nothing by medling with him, although he hath depriued him. My tale is of his depriuation, which was after this sort. The good quiet people of Sydborough, being troubled for certaine yeares with the sayde Wiggington, and many of them being infected by him with the true knowledge of the gospell, by the worde preached (which is an heresie, that his grace doth mortally abhorre and persecute) at length grew in disliking with their pastor, because the seuere man did vrge nothing but obedience vnto the gospell. Well, they came to his grace to finde a remedie hereof: desiring him that Wiggington might be depriued. His grace could find no law to depriue him, no although the pastor defied the Archb. to his face, and would giue him no better title then Iohn Whitgift, such buggs words, being in these daies accounted no lesse then high

treason against a Paltripolitan: Though since that time,
I think his grace hath bin well enured to beare the
name of Pope of Lambeth, Iohn Cant. the prelate of
Lambeth, with diuers other titles agreeable to his func-
tion. Well Sidborogh men proceeded against their
pastor, his grace woulde not depriue him, because he
coulde finde no law to warrant him therein, and he will
do little contrary to law, for fear of a premunire, vnles
it be at a dead lift, to depriue a puritan preacher.
Then in deed he will do against lawe, against God, and
against his owne conscience, rather then that heresie of
preaching should preuail. One man of Sidborough,
whose name is Atkinson, was very eger among the rest,
to haue his pastor depriued: and because his grace
woulde not heare them but departed away, this Atkinson desired his grace to resolue him and his neighbours
of one poynt which something troubled them : and that
was, whether his grace or Wiggington were of the deuill.
For quoth he, you are so contrary the one from the
other, that both of you cannot possibly be of God. If
he be of God, it is certaine you are of the deuill, and so
cannot long stand: for he will be your ouerthrowe.
Amen. If you are of God, then he is of the diuell as
wee thinke him to be, and so he being of the deuill,
will not you depriue him? why shoulde you suffer such
a one to trouble the Church. Now if he be of God,
why is your course so contrary to his? and rather, why
do not you follow him, that we may do so to? Truely,
if you do not depriue him, we will thinke him to be of
God, and go home with him, with gentler good will

towardes him, then we came byther with hatred, and
looke you for a fall. His grace hearing this northen
logicke, was mooued on the sodaine you must thinke,
promised to depriue Wiggington, and so he did. This
Atkinson this winter 1587. came vp to London, being
as it seemed afflicted in conscience for this fact, desired
Wiggington to pardone him and offred to kneele before
her Maiestie, that Wiggington might bee restored againe
to his place, and to stande to the trueth hereof, to his
graces teeth. The man is yet aliue, he may be sent
for, if you thinke that M. Martin hath reported an vn-
trueth. No I warrant you, you shall not take mee to
haue fraught my booke with lyes and slaunders, as Iohn
Whitgift, and the Deane of Sarum did theirs. I speak
not of things by heresay as of reports, but I bring my
witnesses to prooue my matters.

May it please you to yeeld vnto a suite that I haue
to your worships. I pray you send Wiggington home
vnto his charge againe, I can tell you it was a foule
ouersight in his grace, to send for him out of the North
to London, that he might outface him at his owne doore.
He woulde do his Canterburines lesse hurt if he were at
his charge, then now he doth. Let the Templars haue
M. Trauers their preacher restored againe vnto them,
hee is nowe at leysure to worke your priesthood a woe
I hope. If suche another booke as the Ecclesiast. Discipline was, drop out of his budget, it were as good for
the Bb. to lie a day and a night in little ease in the
Counter. He is an od fellowe in folowing an argument,
and you know he hath a smooth tong, either in Latine

or English. And if my L. of Winchester vnderstood, eyther Greeke or Hebrew, as they say he hath no great skill in neyther: I woulde pray your priesdomes to tell me which is the better scholler, Walter Trauers, or Thomas Cooper. Will you not send M. Wyborne to Northampton, that he may see some fruits of the seed he sowed there 16. or 18. yeares ago. That old man Wiborne, hath more good learning in him, and more fit gifts for the ministery in his little toe, then many braces of our Lord Bb. Restore him to preaching againe for shame. M. Paget shalbe welcome to Deuonshire, he is more fit to teach men then boyes. I marueile with what face a man that had done so much good in the Churche as he did among a rude people, could be depriued.

Except persecuting Greenefielde.

Briefely, may it please you to let the Gospell haue a free course, and restore vnto their former libertie in preaching, all the preachers that you haue put to silence: and this far is my first suit.

My 2. suit is a most earnest request vnto you, that are the hinderers of the publishing of the confutation of the Rhemish Testament by M. Cartwright, may be published. A resonable request, the granting whereof, I dare assure you, would be most acceptable vnto all that feare God, and newes of wofull sequell vnto the papists. For shall I tell you what I heard once, from the mouth of a man of great learning and deepe iudgement, who sawe some part of Master Cartwrights answere to the sayde Rhemish and trayterous Raffodie? His iudgment was this. That M. Cartwright had dealt so soundly against the papists, that for the answering and confuting of the aduersary, that one worke woulde be sufficient alone. He farther added, that ye aduersary was confuted by strange and vnknown reasons, that would set them at their wits end, when they see themselues assayled with such weapons, whereof they neuer once drempt, that they should be stroken at. And wil your grace or any els, that are the hinderers of the publishing of this worke, still bereaue the Church of so worthy a Iewell: nay, so strong an armour against the enemie. If you deny me this request, I will not threaten you, but my brother Bridges, and Iohn Whitgiftes bookes shall smoke for this geare, ile haue my peniworths of them for it.

Now may it please you to examine my worthines your brother Martin, and see whether I saide not true in the storie of Gyles Wiggington, where I haue set downe, y^t the preaching of the word is an heresie, which his grace doth mortally abhorre and persecute, I can prooue it without doubt. And first that he persecuteth the preaching of the worde (whether it be an heresie or not) both in the preacher and the hearer: the articles of subscription, the silencing of so many learned and worthy preachers do euidently shew, and if you doubt hereof, let my worshipp vnderstand thereof, and in my next treatize, I shal proue the matter to be cleare with a witnes, and I hope to your smal commendations, that will deny such a cleare point. On the other side, that he accounteth preaching to be an heresie, I am now to insist on the proofe of that poynt. But first you must know, that he did not account simple preaching to be an heresie, but to holde that preaching is the onely ordinary meanes to saluation, this he accounteth as an heresie, this he mortally condemned. The case thus stoode, Iohn Penrie the welsheman (I thinke his grace and my brother London, would be better acquain[ted] with him and they could tell howe) about the beginning of Lent, 1587. offered a supplication and a booke to the Parliament, entreating that some order might be taken, for calling his countrie vnto the knowledge of God. For his bolde attempt, he was called before his grace with others of the high commission, as Thomas of Winchester, Iohn London, &c. After that his grace had eased his stomacke in calling him boy, knaue, varlet, slanderer, libeller, lewde boy, lewd slaunderer, &c. (this is true, for I haue seene the notes of their conference) at the length a poynt of his booke began to be examined, where nonresidents are thought intollerable. Here the Lorde of good London asked M. Penrie, what he could say against that kinde of cattell, aunswere was made that they were odious in the sight of God and man, because as much as in them lie, they bereaue the people ouer whom they thrust themselues, of the ordinarie meanes of saluation, which was the word preached. Iohn London demaunded whether preaching was the onely meanes to saluation? Penrie answered, that it was the onely ordinarie meanes, although the Lorde was not so tyed vnto it, but that hee could extraordinarily vse other meanes. That preaching was the onely ordinary meanes, he confirmed it by those places of scripture, Rom. 10.

14. 1 Cor. 1. 21. Ephes. 1. 13. This point being a
long time canuassed, at the lēgth his worship of Winchester rose vp, and mildly after his manner, brast forth
into these words. I assure you my Lords, it is an exe-
crable beresie: An heresie (quoth Iohn Penry) I thanke
God that euer I knewe that heresie: It is such an
heresie, that I will by the grace of God, sooner leaue
my life then I will leaue it. What sir, (quoth the
Archb.) I tell thee it is an heresie, and thou shalt
recant it as an heresie? Naye (quoth Penrie) neuer so
long as I liue godwilling. I will leaue this storie for
shame, I am weary to hear your grace so absurd. What
say you to this geare my masters of the confocation
house? we shal haue shortly a good religion in England
among the bishops? if Paule be sayd of them to write
an heresie. I haue hard some say, that his grace will
speake against his own conscience? It is true. The
proofe whereof shalbe his dealing with another welshman, one M. Euans. An honorable personage, Ambrose
Dudley, nowe Earle of Warwicke (and long may he be
so, to the glorie of God, the good of his Church, and
the comfort of al his) in the singular loue he bare to the
town of Warwick, would haue placed M. Euans there.
To the ende that master Euans might be receiued with a
fauorable subscription, &c. he offered the subscription
which the Stat. requireth (wherevnto men may subscribe
with a good conscience): The earl sent him with his
letter, to his gracelesnes of Cant. thinking to obtaine so
smal a curtesy at his hands. And I am sure, if he be
Ambrose Dudley, the noble Earle of Warwicke (whose

famous exploytes, both in peace and war, this whole land hath cause to remember with thankfulnes) y^t he is able to requite your kindnes, M. Iohn Cant. O said his grace to M. Euans, I knowe you to be worthy a better place then Warwicke is, and I would very gladly gratifie my Lord, but surely, there is a Lord in heuen whom I feare, and therefore I cannot admit you without subscription. Thus the man with his poore patrone, the earle of Warwick, were reiected by your grace, and the poore earle to this day, knoweth not how to finde the fauour at your hands, that the man may be placed there. I tell you true Iohn Canter. If I were a noble man, and a Counsellor to, I should be sicke of the splene : nay I could not beare this at your hands, to be vsed of a priest thus, contrary to the law of God and this land. It is no maruell though his honor could not obtaine this small suit at your graceles hands, for I haue hearde your owne men say, that you will not be beholding to neuer a noble man in this land, for you were the 2. person, &c. Nay your own selfe spake proudly, yea and that like a pope : when as a worthy knight was a suter vnto your holines, for one of Gods deare children (whom you haue kept and do keepe in prison) for his libertie. You answered him he should lie there stil, vnles he would put in sureties vpon such bonds as neuer the like were hard of: and said further, that you are the 2. person in the land, and neuer a noble man, nor Counsellor in this lande should release him: Onely her Maiestie may release him, and that you were sure, shee would not.

O Monstrous hypocrite.

Doe you thinke this to be he (I pray you) that was sometime doctor Pernes boy, and carried his cloak-bagg after him? Beleeue me he hath leapt lustily? And do not you knowe that after it is full sea, there followeth an eb? Remember your brother Haman? Do you think there is neuer a Mordecai to step to our Gracious Hester, for preseruing the lines of her faithfullest and best subiects, whō you so mortally hate, and bitterly persecute? I hope you haue not long to raigne. Amen. And you M. bishop of Worcester, how delt you with master Evans in the same case? Do you thinke that I do not know your knauerye? you could by law require no other subscription of master Evans then he offered, and yet forsoth, you would not receiue it at his handes, vnlesse he woulde also enter into a bonde, to obscrue the booke of common prayer in euerie poynt, will law permit you to play the tyrant in this sort bishop? I shall see the premunire on the bones of you one day for these pranks. And the masmonger your neighbor the B. of Glocester, thinks to go free, because in his sermon at Paules crosse, preached 1586. in the Parliament time, he affirmed, that beefe and brewesse had made him a papist. But this will not serue his turne: woulde you know what he did? why he conuented an honest draper of Glocester, one Singleton, and vrged him being a lay mā to subscribe vnto the booke. The man affirming that no such thing cold be required of him by law, denied to subscribe: Vpon his deniall the B. sent him to prison. Is it euen so, you old popish priest? dare

Is not this ambitious wretche at the highest thinke you.

you imprison lay men for not subscribing? It were not good for your corner cap that her maiestie knew her subiects to be thus delt with. And if this be euer made knowen vnto her, I hope to see you in for a bird. But brother Winchester, you of all other men are most wretched, for you openly in the audience of many hundreds, at sir Marie Oueries church the last lent, 1587. pronounced that men might finde fault, if they were O blasphem- disposed to quarrell, as well with the Scrip-
ous wretche. ture, as with the booke of Common praier. Who coulde heare this comparison without trembling. But lest you should thinke, that he hath not as good a gift in speaking against his conscience, as my L. of Cant. is endued with: you are to vnderstand, that both in that sermon of his, and in another which he preached at the court the same Lent, he protested before God, A flattering and the congregation where he stood, y^t there
hypocrit. was not in the world at this day: nay there had not bin since the Apostles time, such a flourishing estate of a Church, as we haue now in England. Is it any maruaile that we haue so many swine, dumbe dogs, nonresidents, with their iourneimen the hedge priests, so many lewd liuers, as theeues, murtherers, adulterers, drunkards, cormorants, raschals, so many ignorant and atheistical dolts, so many couetous popish Bb. in our ministery: and so many and so monstrous corruptions in our Church, and yet likely to haue no redresse: Seeing our impudent, shamelesse, and wainscote faced bishops, like beasts, contrary to the knowledge of all men, and against their own consciences, dare in the eares of her

Maiestie, affirme all to be well, where there is nothing
but sores and blisters, yea where the grief is euen deadly
at the heart. Nay saies my L. of Winchester (like a
monstrous hypocrite, for he is a very duns, not able to
defende an argument, but till he come to the pinch, he
will cog and face it out, for his face is made of seasoned
wainscot, and wil lie as fast as a dog can trot) I haue
said it, I doe say it, and I haue said it. And say I,
you shall one day answere it (without repentance) for
abusing the Church of God and her Maiestie in this sort.
I would wish you to leaue this villanie, and the rest of
your diuellishe practises against God his saintes, lest
you answere it where your pieuish and chollerick sim-
plicitie will not excuse you. I am ashamed to think
that the Churche of England shoulde haue these wretches
for the eyes thereof, that woulde haue the people content themselues with bare reading onely, and holde that
they may be saued thereby ordinarily. But this is true
of our Bb. and they are afraid that any thing should be
published abrod, whereby the common people should
learne, that the only way to saluation, is by the word
preached. There was the last sommer a little catechisme, made by M. Dauison and printed by Walde-
graue : but before he coulde print it, it must be authorized by the Bb. either Cante. or London, he went to
Cant. to haue it licensed, his grace committed it to
doctor Neuerbegood (Wood) he read it ouer in halfe a
yeare, the booke is a great one of two sheets of paper.
In one place of the booke, the meanes of saluation was
attributed to the worde preached : and what did he

thinke you? he blotted out the word (preached) and would not haue that word printed, so ascribing the way to work mens saluation to the worde read. Thus they doe to suppresse the trueth, and to keep men in ignorance. Iohn Cant. was the first father of this horrible error in our Church, for he hath defended it in print, and now as you haue hard, accounteth the contrary to be heresie. And popish Goodman, Abbot of Westminster, preaching vpon 12. Rom. 1. said, that so much preaching as in some places we haue is an vnreasonable seruice of God. Scribes, Pharises, and hypocrits, that will neither enter in [y]our selues, nor suffer those that will, to enter into heauen.

May it please your Priestdomes to vnderstand, that doctor Cottington Archdeacon of Surrey, being belike bankerout in his owne countrie, commeth to Kingstone vpon Thames of meere good will that he beareth to the towne (I should say, to vserer Haruies good chear and money bags) being out at the heeles with all other vserers, and knowing him to be a professed aduersary to M. Vdall, (a notable preacher of the Gospell, and vehement reprouer of sinne) taketh the aduantage of their controuersie, and hoping to borow some of the vserers money: setteth himself most vehemently against M. Vdall, to do whatsoeuer Haruie the vserer will haue him: and taketh the helpe of his iourniman doctor Hone, the veriest coxcombe that euer wore veluet cap, and an ancient foe to M. Vdall, because (in deed) he is popish dolt, and (to make up a messe) Steuen Chatfield, the vicker of Kingston, as very a bankerout and duns as

Doc. Cottington (although he haue consumed all the money he gathered to build a Colledge at Kingstone) must come and be resident there, that M. Vdall may haue his mouth stopped, and why? forsoth because your friend M. Haruie woulde haue it so: for sayth Haruie, he rayleth in his sermons, is that true? Doth he rail, when he reproueth thee (and such notorious varlets as thou art) for thy vsery, for thy oppressing of the poore, for buying the houses ouer their heads that loue the gospell, and the Lord his faythfull minister? (M. Vdall) And art not thou a monstrous atheist, a belly God, a carnall wicked wretch, and what not. M. Chatfield you thinke I see not your knauery? is vs do I, you cannot daunce so cunningly in a net but I can spie you out? shal I tel you why you sow pillows vnder Haruies elbowes? Why man, it is because you would borow an 100. pound of him? Go to you Asse, and take in M. Vdall againe (for Haruie I can tell, is as craftie a knane as you, he will not lend his money to such bankerouts, as Duns Cottington and you are) and you do not restore M. Vdall againe to preach, I will so lay open your vilenes, y^t I will make the very stoones in Kingstone streets shall smell of your knaueries. Nowe if a man aske M. Cottington why M. Vdall is put to silence? forsoth saith he, for not fauoring the Churche gouernement present. Doc. Hone (Cottingtons iourniman, a popish D. of the baudy court) saith by his troth, for making such variance in the town. M. Chatfield seemeth to sorie for it, &c. But what cause was alleaged why M. Vdall must preach no longer? surely this onely? that he had not my L. of Winchesters licence vnder seale to shew : and because this was thought not to be sufficient to satisfie the people : Hone the baudie Doctor, charged him to be a sectarie, a schismatike, yea he affirmed plainly, that the gospell out of his mouth was blasphemie. Popish Hone, do you say so? do ye? you are a knaue I tel you? by ye same token your friend Chatfield spent thirteene score pounds in distributing briefes, for a gathering towards the erecting of a Colledge at Kingstone upon Thames.

Wohohow, brother London, do you remember Thomas Allen and Richard Alworth, marchants of London, being executors to George Allen somtimes your grocer, but now deceased: who came vnto you on easter wednesday last being at your masterdoms pallace in Londō, hauing bene often to speake with you before and could not, yet now they met with you: who tolde you they were excutors vnto one George Allen (somtimes) your grocer, and among other his debts, we finde you indebted vnto him, in the some of 19. pound and vpward, desiring you to let them haue the money, for that they were to dispose of it according to that trust he reposed in them. You answered them sweetly (after you had pawsed a while) in this manner: You are raskals, you are villaines, you are arraunt knaues, I owe you nought, I haue a generall quittance to shew. Sir (sayd they) shew vs your discharge, and we are satisfied. No (quoth he) I will shew you none, go sue me, go sue me. Then sayd one of the merchants, doe you thus vse vs for asking our due? Wee

Can B. face, cog lie and cosen or no thinke you.

would you should know, we are no suche vile persons.
Done Iohn of London (hearing their answere) cried out,
saying: Hence away, Citizens? nay you are
raskcals, you are worse then wicked mam-
mon (so lifting vp both his hands, and flinging
them downe againe, said) You are theeues, you are
Coseners: take that for a bishops blessing, and so get
you hence. But when they would haue aunswered, his
men thrust them out of the dores. But shortly after,
he perceiued they went about to bring the matter to
farther tryial: he sent a messenger vnto them confessing
the debt, but they cannot get their money to this day.
What reason is it they should haue their mony? hath he
not bestowed his liberallitie alreadie on them? Can
they not be satisfied with the blessing of this braue
bounsing priest? But brethren bishops, I pray you tell
me? hath not your brother Londō, a notable brazen
face to vse these men so for their owne? I told you,
Martin will be proued no lyar, in that he saith that
Bb. are cogging and cosening knaues. This priest went
to buffets with his sonne in law, for a bloodie nose,
well fare all good tokens. The last lent there came a
commaundement from his grace into Paules Churchyard,
that no Byble should be bounde without the Apocripha.
Monstrous and vngodly wretches, that to maintaine their
owne outragious proceedings, thus mingle heauen and
earth together, and woulde make the spirite of God, to
be the author of prophane bookes. I am hardly drawn
to a merie vaine from such waightie matters.

But you see my worshipfull priestes of this crue to

Dumbe Iohn of Londōs blessing.

whom I write, what a perilous fellow M. Marprelate is:
he vnderstands of all your knauerie, and it may be he
keepes a register of them: vnlesse you amend, they
shall al come into the light one day. And you brethren
bishops, take this warning from me. If you doe not
leaue your persecuting of godly christians and good
subiectes, that seeke to liue vprightly in the feare of
God, and the obedience of her Maiestie, all your dealing shalbe made knowen vnto the world. And ise be
sure to make you an example to all posterities. You
see I haue taken some paynes with you alreadie, and
I will owe you a better turne, and pay it you with
aduauntage, at the least thirteene to the dozen, vnles
you obserue these conditions of peace which I drawe
betweene me and you. For I assure you, I make not
your doings known for anie mallice that I beare vnto
you, but the hurt that you doe vnto Gods Churche,
leaue you your wickednesse, and ile leaue the reuealing
of your knaueries.

☞ *Conditions of Peace to be inuiolablie kept for euer,
betweene the reuerend and worthy master Martin Marprelate gentleman on the one partie, and the reuerend
fathers his brethren, the Lord bishops of this lande.*

1. *In primis*, the said Lord Bb. must promise and
obserue, without fraud or collusion, and that as much as
in them lyeth, they labor to promote the preaching of
the worde in euery part of this land.

2. That hereafter they admitt none vuto the minis-

terie, but such as shalbe knowen, both for their godlinesse and learning, to be fit for the ministerie, and not these neyther without cure, vnlesse they be Colledge ministers of eyther of the Vniuersities, and in no case they suffer any to be nonresidents: and that they suffer M. Cartwrightes answere to the Rhemish Testament to be published.

3. That neyther they nor their seruants, vz. their Archdeacons, Chancellors, nor any other of the high commission, which serue their vile affections, vrge any to subscribe contrary to the statute 13. Eliza. and that they suspend or silence none, but such, as either for their false doctrine, or euill life, shall shew themselues, to be vnworthy the places of ministers: so that none be suspended or silenced, eyther for speaking (when their text giueth them occasion) against the corruptions of the Church, for refusing to weare the surplice, cap, tippet, &c. or omitting the corruptions of the booke of common prayers, as churching of women, the crosse in baptisme, the ring in marriage, &c.

4. That none be molested by them or any their aforesaid seruants, for this my booke, for not kneeling at the communion, or for resorting on the Saboth (if they haue not preachers of their owne) to heare the word preached, and to receiue the Sacraments.

5. Lastly, that neuer hereafter they profane excommunication as they haue done, by excommunicating alone in their chambers, and that for trifles: yea before mens causes be heard. That they neuer forbid publike fasts, molest either preacher, or hearer, for being present

at such assemblies. Briefly, that they neuer slander the cause of reformation, or the furtherers thereof, in terming the cause by the name of Anabaptisterie, schisme, &c. and the men puritans, and enemies to the state.

These be the conditions, which you brethren bishops, shalbe bound to keepe inuiolably on your behalfe. And I your brother Martin on the other side, do faithfully promise vpon the performaunce of the premisses by you, neuer to make any more of your knauery knowne vnto the worlde. And howbeit that I haue before threatened my brother Bridges, in the cause of his superior priest, and your Antichristian callings: notwithstanding, I will write no more of your dealings, vnles you violate the former conditions. The conditions you see, are so reasonable, I might binde you to giue ouer your places which are Antichristian: but I doe not, lest men shoulde thinke me to quarrell, and seeke occasions for the nonce to fall out with my brethrē. Therefore I require no more but such things as all the worlde will thinke you vnworthy to liue, if you grant them not. And this I doe the rather, because you should not, according to your olde fashion, say y^t my worship doth for mallice lay opē your infirmities: nay I haue published not one of your secret falts, what you haue not blushed to commit in the face of the sun, and in the iustfiing whereof you yet stand, these things onely haue I published. The best seruants of God I know, haue their infirmities. But none of thē will stand in the maintenance of their corruptions as you do, and that to the dishonour of God and the ruine of his Church. You must either amend, or shortly you will bring our church to ruine : therfore it is time that your dealings were better looked vnto.

You will go about I know, to proue my booke to be a libell, but I haue preuented you of y^t aduantage in lawe, both in bringing in nothing but matters of fact, whiche may easily be prooued, if you dare denie them ; and also in setting my name to my booke. Well I offer you peace vpon the former conditions, if you will keepe them, but if you violate thē either in whole or in part (for why should you breake anye one of them) then your learned brother Martin doth proclaime open war against you, and entendeth to worke your woe 2. maner of wayes as followeth. First I will watch you at euery halfe turne, and whatsoeuer you do amisse, I will presently publish it : you shall not call one honest man before you, but I will get his examination (and you thinke I shall knowe nothing of the oppression of your tenants by your briberie, &c.) and publish it, if you deal not according to the former conditions. To this purpose I wil place a yong Martin in euerie diocesse, which may take notice of you practizes. Do you think that you shalbe suffred any longer, to break the law of God, and to tyrannize ouer his people her Maiesties subiectes, and no man tell you of it? No I warrant you. And rather then I will be disappointed of my purpose, I will place a Martin in euerie parish. In part of Suffolk and Essex, I thinke I were best to haue 2. in a parishe. I hope in time they shalbe as worthie Martins as their father is, euery one of them able to mar a prelate. Marke what wil be the issue of these things, if you still keep your olde byas. I knowe you would not haue your dealings so knowne vnto the worlde, as I and my sonnes will blase them. Secondly, al the books that I haue in store already of your doings, shalbe published vpon the breache of the former couenants or any of them. Here I know some will demand what these bookes are, because saith one, I warrant you, there will be old sport, I hope olde father Palinod D. Perne, shall be in there by the weekes. Why my masters of the cleargie, did you neuer heare of my books in deed? Foe, then you neuer heard of good sport in your life. The catalogue of their names, and the arguments of some are as followeth. As for my booke named "Epistomastix," I make no mention thereof at this time. First my "Paradoxes," 2. my "Dialogues," 3. my "Miscelanea," 4. my "Variæ leiciones," 5. "Martins dreame," 6. "Of the liues and doings of English popes," 7. my "Itinerarium, or visitations," 8. my "Lambathismes." In my "Paradoxes" shalbe handled som points, which the cōmon sort haue not greatly considered of: as 1 That our prelates, if they professed popery, could not do so much hurt vnto Gods Church as now they do. 2 That the Diuell is not better practized in bowling and swering then Iohn of London is, with other like points. What shalbe handled in my 2. 3. 4. 5. and 6. bookes, you shall know when you read them.

Mine Epitome is readie.

Mine "Iterarium" shalbe a booke of no great profit, eyther to the Church or commonwealth: and yet had nede to be in follio, or else iudge you by this that fol-

loweth. I meane to make a suruey into all the diocesse
in this land, that I may keepe a visitation among my
cleargie men. I would wish them to keepe good rule,
and to amend their manners against I come. For I
shall paint them in their coulers, if I finde any thing
amisse: In this booke I wil note all their memorable
pranckes. As for example, if I finde anye priest to
haue done as Sir Gefferie Iones of Warwicke shire did,
that must be set downe in my visitations, and I thinke
I had need to haue many Scribes, and many reames of
paper for this purpose. The said sir Iefferie Iones,
committed a part verie well beseeming his priesthood,
which was after this maner. Sir Ieffry once in an alehouse (I doe desire the reader to beare with me, though
according to M. Bridges his fashion, I write false Englishe in this sentence) whereunto he resorted for his
morning draught, either because his hostesse woulde
haue him pay the olde score before he should run any
further, or the new, or els because the gamesters his
companions wan all his monie at trey trip: tooke such
vnkindenes at the alehouse, that he sware he would
neuer goe againe into it. Although this rash vow of
the good priest, was made to the great losse of the ale-
wife, who by means of sir Iefferie was woont to haue
good vtterance for her ale: yet I think the tap had
great quietnes and ease therby, which coulde not be
quiet so much as an houre in the day, as long as Sir
Iefferie resorted vnto the house, how sweete it was,
poore sir Iones felt the discommoditie of his rashe vowe.
Then alas, he was in a woe case, as you know: for his

stomacke could not be at all strengthened with the drink he got abroad. But better were a man not to feele his discommoditie, then not to be able to redresse the same. Therefore at length sir Iefferie bethought him of a feat whereby he might both visit the alestond, and also keepe his othe. And so he hired a man to carie him vpon his backe to the alehouse, by this meanes he did not goe, but was caried thither, wherevnto he made a vow neuer to go. I doubt not in my visitation, but to get a hundreth of these stratagemes, especially if I trauell neere where any of the vickers of hell are. As in Surrie, Northampton, and Oxforde shires. And I would wish the Purcivants and the Stacioners, with the Woolfe their beadle, not to be so redy to molest honest men. And Stacioners, I would wish you not to be so francke with your bribes, as you were to Thomas Draper, I can tell you his grace had need to prouide a bag ful of Items for you, if you be so liberal. Were you so foolish (or so malicious against Walde-graue) to giue that knaue Draper fiue pounds to betray him into your wretched hands: he brought you to Kingstone vpon Thames, with Purcivants to take him, where he should be a printing books in a Tinkars house: (your selues being disguised so, that Walde-graue might not know you, for of Citizens you were becom ruffians). There you were to seek that could not be found, and many such iournies may you make. But when you came to London, you laid Thomas Draper in the Counter for cosenage. O well bowlde, when Iohn of London throwes his bowle, he will runne after it, and crie rub, rub, rub, and say the diuill go with thee. But what thinke you shalbe handled in my "Lambathismes?" Truely this, I will there make a comparison of Iohn Whitgifts Canterburines, with Iohn Bridges his Lambathismes. To speake in plaine English, I will there set downe the flowers of errors, popishe and others, wherewith those two worthie men haue stuffed the bookes which they haue written against the cause of reformation, in the defence of the gouernment of Bb. I haue in this book as you shal see, gathered some flowers out of Iohn of Londons booke, but my "Lambathismes" shalbe done otherwise I trow.

And now if it may please you of the Confocationhouse, to here of any of the former books, then break the league which I offer to make with you, but if you woulde haue my friendship, as I seeke yours, then let me see that you persecute no more, and especially, that you trouble none for this booke of mine. For this must be an especiall article of our agreement, as you know. And Deane Iohn, for your part, you must plaie the fool no more in the pulpit : we will end this matter with a prettie storie of a certaine mischance that befell a B. corner cap, as followeth. Olde doctor Turner (I meane not D. Perne the old turner) had a dog full of good quallities. D. Turner hauing inuited a B. to his table, in dinner while called his dog, and told him that the B. did sweat (you must think he labored hard ouer his trencher) The dogg flies at the B. and tooke of his corner capp (he thought belike it had bene a cheese cake) and so away goes the dog with it to his master. Truely my masters of the cleargie, I woulde neuer weare corner cap againe, seeing dogs runne away with them: and here endeth the storie.

May it please you that are of this house, to tell me the cause, when you haue leysure, why so many opinions and errors are risen in our Church, concerning the ministery, and the ioyning with preaching and vnpreaching ministers. To tell you my opinion in your eare, I thinke it to be want of preaching, and I thinke your worships to haue bene the cause of all this stir. Some puritans holde readers for no ministers, som hold you our worthy Bb. for little better then faire parchment readers, and say that you haue no learning. Now whether readers be ministers or no, and whether our bishops be learned or no, I woulde wish you brethren bishops, and you brethren puritans, to make no great controuersie, but rather labor that all euil ministers may be turned out of the Church, and so I hope there shoulde be a speedie ende of all those questions betweene you. For then I doubt not, but that Lord bishops whereat the puritans so repine, shoulde be in a faire reckoning within short space, euen the next to the dore saue the dog: and I see that you bishopps are well towardes this promotion alreadie. And truely, though the puritans should neuer so much repine at the matter, yet I tell you true, I am glad that you are so esteemed among mē. And for mine owne part, I think my masters, that manie of you our Lord Bb. and cleargie men, are men verie notorious for their learning and preaching. And hereof vnder Benedicite betweene you and me, (the puritanes may stand aside nowe) I will bring you some instances.

First his grace and my L. of Winchester haue bene verie notable clarkes, euer since M. doctor Sparke set them at a *non plus* (some of their honors being present) in the conference betweene him and M. Trauers on the puritans side, and the two Archbishops and the B. of Winchester on the other side. D. Sparks argument was drawn from the corruption of the translation of the 28. verse of the 105. Psalme, in the booke of Common prayer, and the contrarietie of the translations allowed by the Bb. themselues. For in the book of Common prayer you shal read thus: And they were not obedient vnto his word (which is a plain corruptiō of the text) in other priuiledged English translations it is, And they were not disobedient vnto his word, which is according to the veritie of the originall. By the way ere I go any further, I would know with what conscience, either my brother Cant. or any els of our Bb. can vrge men to allow such palpable corruptions by subscribing vnto thinges meere contrarie to the word. Here also I would shew by the way, and I woulde haue al my sonnes to note, that their vncle Canterburies drift in vrging subscription, is not the vnity of the church (as he would pretende) but the maintenance of his owne pride and corruption, which should soon come to ye ground, if the worde had free passage: and therefore he prooueth the same, by stopping the mouthes of ye sincere preachers thereof. For if the vnitie of the Church had bene his end, why hath not he amended this fault in all the books that haue bene printed since that time, which now is not so little as 3 yeares, in which time, many thousand of

books of Common praier haue bin printed. If he had
other busines in hand then the amending of the booke of
Common prayer? why had he not, nay why doth he not
leaue vrging of subscription vntill that be amended?
Can he and his hirelings haue time to imprison and
depriue men, because they will not sinne, by approuing
lyes vpon the holy ghost (which thinges they cannot,
nor could not chuse but commit, whosoeuer will or haue
subscribed vnto the booke and Articles) And can he
haue no time in 3. or 4. yeares to correct most grose
and vngodly faultes in the print, whereof the putting
out of one syllable, enen three letters (dis) would haue
amended this place. But it lieth not in his grace to
amende the corruptions of the booke. Belike it lieth in
him to doe nothing but sinne, and to compell men
against their consciences to sinne, or else to bring
extreme miserie vpon them. If it laye not in him, yet
he might haue acquainted the Parliament (for there was
a Parliament since the time he knew this fault) with the
corruptions of the booke. And I will come neerer home
to him then so, in the Article concerning the gouernment
whereunto men are vrged to subscribe. You must (say
the Articles) protest that there is nothing in the ministery of the Church of England, that is not according
to ye word, or to such like effect they speake. I say
that I cannot subscribe vuto this article, because contrary to the expresse commandement of our sauiour
Christ, and the examples of his Apostles, there be Lords
in ye ministerie, or such as wold be accoūted ministers,
will also be called and accoūted Lords, and bear ciuill

offices, the words of Christ are those. The kinges of
the Gentils raigne ouer them, and they that beare rule
ouer them, are called gracious Lords, but you shall not
be so, Luk. 22. 25. 26. I saye that out of this place,
it is manifest, that it is vtterly vnlawfull for a minister
to be a Lord: that is, for any L. B. to be in the ministerie : and therefore I cannot subscribe vnto that Article
which would haue me iustifie this to be lawfull. Nowe
I will cease this point, because I doubt not but the
Articles of subscription, wilbe shortly so made out of
fashion, that the Bb. will be ashamed of them themselues: and if no other will take them in hande, ile
turne one of mine owne breede vnto them, eyther Martin senior, or some of his brethren.

To go forward, his Lordship of Winchester is a great
Clarke, for he hath translated his Dictionarie, called
Copers Dictionarie, verbatim out of Robert Stephanus
his Thesaurus, and ilfauored to they say. But what
do I speake of our bishops learning, as long as bishop
Ouerton, bishopp Bickley, bishop Middleton, the Deane
of Westminster, doctor Cole, D. Bell, with many others,
are liuing, I doubt me whether all the famous dunses be
dead. And if you woulde haue an ilsample of an excel-
lent pulpit man in deede, go no further then the B. of
Glocester nowe lining: And in him you shall finde a
plaine instance of such a one as I meane. On a time
he preaching at Worcester before he was B. vpon Sir
Iohns day: as he trauersed his matter, and discoursed
vpon many points, he came at the length vnto the very
pithe of his whol sermon, contained in the distinction of

the name of Iohn, which he then shewing all his learning at once, full learnedly handled after this manner. Iohn, Iohn, the grace of God, the grace of God, the grace of God: gracious Iohn, not graceles Iohn, but gracious Iohn. Iohn, holy Iohn, holy Iohn, not Iohn ful of holes, but holy Iohn. If he shewed not himselfe learned in this sermond, then hath he bene a duns all his life. In the same sermon, two seuerall Iohns, the father and the sonne, that had beene both recusants, being brought publikely to confesse their faults, this worthy doctor, by reason that the yong man hauing bene poysoned beyond the seas with popery, was more obstinate then his father, and by all likelihood, he was ye cause of his fathers peruersenesse: with a vehement exclamatiō, able to pearce a cobweb, called on the father aloud in this patheticall and perswading sort. Old Iohn, olde Iohn, be not led away by the Syren sounds, and inticements of yong Iohn, if yong Iohn will go to the diuell, the diuell go with him. The puritans it may be, will here obiect, that this worthy man was endued with these famous gifts before he was B. whereas since that time, say they, he is not able to say bo to a goose. You wey this man belike my masters, according to the rest of our Bb. But I assure you it is not so with him. For the last Lent in a sermon he made in Glocester towne, he shewed him selfe to be the man that he was before. For he did in open pulpit confirme the trueth of his text to be authenticall, being the prophesie of Isaiah, out of the book of Cōmon prayer, whiche otherwise would (it is to be feared) haue proued Apocrypha.

His text was, a childe is borne vnto vs, which after he sweetly repeated very often as before, to the great destruction and admiration of the hearers, saying : A child is borne, a child is borne, a child is borne vnto vs this (sayth he) is proued you know, where in that worthy verse of the booke of Common prayer. Thy honorable true and onely sonne. Afterward, repeating the same words againe : A childe is borne vnto vs, a childe is borne vnto vs: here sayth hee, I might take occasion to commende that worthy verse in our Latenie, where this is made very manifest, that ye prophet here speaketh. By thy Natiuitie and circumcision. What should I prosecute the condemnation of this man, as though other our Bb. and pulpit men haue not as commendable gifts as he.

And once againe to you brother Bridges, you haue set downe a flanting reason, in the 75. page of your book, against the continuance of the gouernment which the Puritans labor for, and I finde the same syllogisme concluded in no mood : therefore what if I was ashamed to put it downe ? But seeing it is your will, to laye on the puritans with it as it is, put your corner cap a litle nere a toe side, that we may see your partie coullered beard, and with what a manly countenance, you giue your brethren this scouring. And I hope this will please you, my cleargie masters, as well as if I tolde you how our brother Bridges plaid my L. of Winchesters foole, in sir Maries pulpit in Cambridg, but no word of that : now to my reason.

Some kinde of ministerie ordained by the Lorde, was

temporarie (saith he) as for example, the Mosaicall priesthood, and the ministerie of Apostles, prophets, &c. But the ministerie of pastors, doctors, elders and deacons, was ordayned by the Lord: Therefore it was temporarie.

Alacke, alacke deane Iohn, what haue you done now? The puritanes will be O the bones of you too badd, for this kinde of arguing, and they wil reason after this sort.

1 Some man in the land (say they) weareth a wooden dagger and a coxcombe, as for example, his grace of Canterburies foole, doctor Pernes cosen and yours: you presbyter Iohn Catercap, are some man in the land: Therefore by this reason, you wear a woodden dagger and a coxcombe. 2 Some presbyter prieste or elder in the English ministerie, is called the vicker of hell. As for example one about Oxford, another neere Northampton, and the parson of Micklaim in Surrie: But the dean of Sarum Iohn Catercap, is some priest in the Englishe ministerie: Ergo he is the vicker of hell. 3 Some presbyter priest or elder, preaching at Pauls crosse 1587. tould a tale of a leadden shoinghorne, and spake of Catekissing: and preaching at the Court on another time, thrust his hand into his pocket, and drew out a piece of sarsnet, saying, behold a relique of Maries smocke: and thrusting his hand into the other pocket, drew out either a linnen or a wollen rag, saying, behold a relique of Iosephs breeches. But quoth he, there is no reason why Maries smocke shoulde be of sarsnet, seeing Iosephs breeches were not of silke. This prist

being lately demanded whether he should be bishop of Eli, answered that he had now no great hope to B. of Eli : and therefore quoth he, I may say well inough, Eli, Eli, Lammasabacthani. Eli, Eli, why hast thou forsaken me. Alluding very blasphemously vnto the words which our Sauiour Christe spake, in his greatest agonie vpon the crosse. The same priest calling before him one M. Benison a preacher, and would haue vrged him to take his othe, to answere to such articles as he would propounde against him, who answered saying, brother bishop, I wil not sweare, except I know to what? with that the priest fell sicke of the splene, and began to sweare by his fayth: quoth Benison, a Bishop should preache fayth, and not sweare by it. This priest being in his malancholicke mood, sent him to the Clincke, where he lay till her Maiestie was made priuie of his tyrannie, and then released to the priests wo. As for example, the B. of Londoo did al those things and more to : For lying at his house at Haddam in Essex, vpon the Sabboth day (wanting his bowling mates) tooke his seruantes and went a heymaking, the godly ministers round about being exercised (though against his commandement) in fasting and prayer : But you Iohn Catercap, are some presbyter priest or Elder : Therefore you prophaned the word and ministerie in this sort. 4 Some presbyter priest or elder in the land, is accused (and euen now the matter is in triall before his grace and his brethren) to haue two wiues, and to marie his brother vnto a woman vpon her death bedd, shee being past recouerie. As for example, the B. of sir Dauies in

Wales, is this priest as they saye: But you presbyter Iohn, are some priest: Therefore you haue committed all these vnnaturall parts. 5 Some priest preaching at the funeralls of one who died, not onely being condemned by the lawe of God and of the land, for attempting matters against her Maiesties person and the state, but also dyed an obstinate and professed papist, and without anye repentance for her enterprises against her Maiestie and the state: prayed that his soule, and the soules of all the rest there present, might be with the soule of the vnrepentant papist departed. As for example, the B. of Lincolne did this at Peterborough, August. 2. 1587. But you are som priest: Ergo you made such a prayer. 6 Some priest in ye land lately made, or verie shortly meaneth to make, as they say, an olde acquaintance of his owne, Richard Patrick, clothier of Worcester, of the reading ministery. As for example, his grace of Canter. is this priest: But you brother Sarum are som priest as wel as he: Ergo you haue thrust a bankerout clothier in the ministerie. 7 Some priest hauing giuen a man (whose wife had plaid the harlot) leaue to marie another, desiring the man long after he had bene maried to another woman, to shewe him his letters of diuorcement, with promise to deliuer them againe: But hauing receiued them, they are retained of him most iniuriously vnto this day, and he troubleth the man for hauing two wiues: as for example, the B. of sir Asse is this priest: But you dean Catercap are som priest: Ergo you do men such open iniurie. 8 Some men that breake the lawe of God are traytors to her Maiestie, as for example, the Iesuites. But all our bishops are some men that breake the law of God, because they continue in vnlawful callings: Ergo by your reason they are traitors to her maiestie, but I deny your argument, for there may be manie breaches of the law of God, whereof they may be guiltie, and yet no traytors. 9 Some men that will not haue their Lordships, and their callings examined by the worde, are limbs of Antichrist, as for example, the Pope and his Cardinals: But our L. bishops are some men which will not haue their lordships and their callings tried by the word: Therefore they are limbs of Antichrist. 10 Some men would play the turncoats, with the B. of Glocester, D. Renold, D. Perne (I wil let D. Goodman Abbot of West. alone now) But all the L. bishops, and you brother catercap are some men: Ergo you would becom papists againe. 11 Some men dare not dispute with their aduersaries, lest their vngodly callings shoulde be ouerthrowen, and they compelled to walke more orderly: But our Bb. are some men: Ergo they dare not dispute lest their vngodly callings and places shoulde be ouerthrowen. 12 Som men are theeues and foul murtherers before God, as for example, all nonresidents: Euerie L. bishop is a nonresident: Ergo he is a thiefe and a foule murtherer before God. 13 Some men are become Apostataes frō their ministerie, sinners against their owne consciences, persecuters of their brethren, sacriligious Church robbers, withstanders of the known trueth, for their owne filthie lukers sake, and are afraid lest the gospel and the holy discipline thereof should be receiued in euerie place: But our Bb. are some men: Therfore (by your reson M. doctor) they are become Apostaes from their ministerie, sinners against their owne consciences, persecutors of their brethren, sacriligious Church robbers, and withstanders of the knowen truth, &c. 14 Som priest is a pope, as for example, that priest which is bishop of Rome is a Pope: But his grace of Cant. is some priest: Therefore M. Bridges, by your maner of reasoning, he is a Pope. You may see what harme you haue done by dealing so loosely. I knowe not what I shall say to these puritans reasons? They must needs be good, if yours be sound. Admit their syllogisms offended in form as yours doth: yet the common people, and especially dame Lawson, and the gentlewoman, whose man demanded of her, whē she sat at the B. of Londons fire: why mistris wil you sit by Caiphas his fire? will finde an vnhappy trueth in many of these conclusions, when as yours is most false. And many of their propositions are tried truths, hauing many eye and eare witnesses liuing.

Men when commonly they dedicate bookes vnto any, enter into commendations of those vnto whom they write. But I care not an I owe you my cleargie masters a commendations, and pay you when you better deserue it. In stead thereof, I will giue you some good counsel and aduice, which if you followe, I assure you it will be the better for you.

First I would aduise you as before I haue said, to set at libertie all the preachers that you haue restrained frō preaching: otherwise it shalbe the worse for you, my reason is this. The people are altogether discontented for want of teachers. Some of them alreadie runne into corners, and more are like, because you keepe the meanes of knowledge from them. Running into corners will breed Anabaptistrie, Anabaptistrie will allienate the heartes of the subiects from their lawfull gouernour. And you are the cause hereof. And wil not her Maiestie then think you, require the hearts of her subiectes at your handes, whē she shal vnderstand that they are alienated (as God forbid they should) from her by your means? yes I warrant you. And if they should put vp a supplication vnto her highnesse, that their preachers might be restored vnto them, I doubt not but they should be heard. I can tell you she tendreth the estate of her people, and will not discourage their hearts, in casting of their suits, to maynetaine your pride and couetousnesse: you were then better to set the preachers at libertie, then to suffer your cruelty and euill dealing to be made known vuto her. For so they shall be sure I doubt not to preuaile in their suit, and you to go by the worse. And try if her Maiestie be not shortly mooued in this suit. To it my masters roundly, you that meane to deale herein, and on my life you set the prelats in such a quandare, as they shal not know wher to stand. Now M. Prelates I will giue you some more counsell, follow it. Repent cleargie men, and especially bishopps, preach fayth Bb. and sweare no more by it, giue ouer your Lordly callings: reform your families and your children: They are the patterne of loosenesse, withstand not the knowen truth no longer:

you haue seduced her Maiestie and her people. Praye her Maiestie to forgiue you, and the Lord first to put away your sinnes. Your gouerment is Antichristian, deceiue the Lord no longer thereby: You wil grow from euil to worse vnlesse betimes you return. You are now worse then you were 29. yeeres ago: write no more against the cause of reformation: Your vngodlinesse is made more manifest by your writings: And because you cannot answer what hath bene written against you, yeeld vnto the trueth. If you should write, deal syllogistically: For you shame your selues, when you vse any continued speach, because your stile is so rude and barbarous. Raile no more in the pulpitt against good men, you do more hurt to your selnes, and your owne desperat cause, in one of your rayling sermons, then you could in speaking for reformation. For euerie man that hath any light of religion in him will examine your groundes, which being found ridiculous (as they are) will be decided, and your cause made odious. Abuse not the high cōmission as you do, against the best subiects. The commission it selfe was ordained for very good purposes, but it is most horriblie abused by you, and turned cleane contrarie to the ende wherefore it was ordayned. Helpe the poore people to the meanes of their saluation, that perish in their ignorance: make restitution vuto your tenants, and such as from whome you haue wrongfully extorted any thing: Vsurpe no longer, the authoritie of making of ministers and excommunication: Let poore men be no more molested in your vngodly courts: Studie more then you doe, and preache oftener : Fauor nonresidents and papists no longer : labor to clense ye ministery of the swarms of ignorant guides, wherewith it hath bin defiled : Make conscience of breaking the Sabboth, by bowling and tabling : Be ringleaders of prophanenes no longer vnto the people : Take no more bribes : Leaue your Symonie : Fauor learning more then you doe, and especially godly learning : Stretch your credit if you haue any to the furtherance of the gospell : You haue ioyned the prophanation of the magistracie, to the corruption of the ministerie : Leaue this sinne. All in a word, become good christians, and so you shall become good subiects, and leaue your tyrannie. And I would aduise you, let me here no more of your euill dealing.

Giuen at my Castle between two Wales, neither foure dayes from penilesse benche, nor yet at the West ende of Shrofftide : but the foureteenth yeare at the least, of the age of Charing crosse, within a yeare of Midsommer, betweene twelue and twelue of the clocke. *Anno pontificatus vestri Quinto,* and I hope *vltimo* of all Englishe Popes.

By your learned and worthie brother,

MARTIN MARPRELATE.

NOTES.

Page 3, line 16. *D. Cosins hath a very good grace in iesting*] The allusion is to the " Abstract of certain Acts of Parliament of certain Injunctions," &c., published in 1584, and which Dr. Cosins replied to by authority of Archbishop Whitgift, in the same year. The Counterpoyson was printed in 1584, which Dr. Copcot answered in a Latin sermon, preached at Paul's Cross, in 1585. The sermon does not appear to have been printed, for the author of " A Defense of the Reasons of the Counterpoyson," 1586, tells us, " the author of the Counterpoyson never could get the answeres *in writing, as nowe I haue got them.* Since that I myself have fallen uppon the *whole sermon in writing,* so that it seemeth it goeth from hand to hande amongst those who delight in it."

P. 3, l. 26. *Cartwrights bookes*] The controversy between Whitgift and Cartwright began in 1572 with the publication of the " Admonition to the Parliament." According to Neal [Hist. Puritans, i. 231. ed. 1822] it was drawn up by Field, a minister, assisted by Wilcox, and revised by others. The authors presented it to the House, for which they were committed to Newgate Oct. 8, 1572. The Admonition was, however, suffered to be printed, and in the course of two years passed through three or four editions. [Strype's Parker, 347.] The imprisonment of Field and Wilcox occasioned the publication of a " Second Admonition," written by Cartwright, and two other tracts, entitled " An Exhortation to the Bishops to deal brotherly with their brethren," and another " Exhortation to the Bishops to answer the Admonition." The bishops, thinking it necessary to reply, appointed Whitgift to the work, and, before it came out, it underwent the revision and correction of Archbishop Parker, Dr. Pern, Bishop of Ely, and Dr. Cooper, Bishop of Lincoln. It was entitled " An Answeare to a certain Libel, entitled *An Admonition to the Parliament,* 1572." Cartwright to this replied in 1573, in " A Replye to an Answere made of Dr. VVhitgifte againste the Admonition to the Parliament." Whitgift then published " The Defence of the Aunswere to the Admonition against the Replie of T. C. 1574." The following year came out, "The Second Replie," and, in 1577, "The Rest of the Second Replie of Thomas Cartvuright agaynst Master Doctor Vuhitgifts Second Ansvuer touching the Church Discipline." To this "Second Replie" no answer was returned, and hence Martin, writing towards the end of 1588, says, "You first prouoked him to write, and you first haue receiued the foyle;" and, in allusion to the same subjcet at p. 22, "For this dozen yeares we neuer saw any thing of his [Whitgift's] in printe for the defence of this cause, and poore M. Cartwright doth content himselfe with the victorie, which the other will not (though in deed he hath by his silence) seeme to grant."

P. 4, l. 13. *quoth John Elmar in his Harborow of faithful subiects.*] Written in reply to John Knox's "first Blast of the Trumpet against the Monstrous Regiment of Women," it is entitled "An Harborowe for Faithful and Trewe Subiects against the late blowne Blast, concerning the Government of Wemen, anno MDlix. Strasborowe the 26 of April."

P. 8, l. 13. *Which Harmonie, was* translated *and printed by that puritan Cambridg printer, Thomas Thomas.*] A new edition of the "Harmony of the Confessions" has recently issued from the press, edited by the Rev. Peter Hall. Its value is much enhanced by the addition of the Articles of the Church of England, 1562, and of Ireland, 1615, the Judgment of the Synod of Dort, and the Westminster Confession, with an Index to the Doctrines in the Harmony. The editor, in a Note appended to the Introduction, has thrown some discredit on the statement that Thomas Thomas was the translator of the Harmony, but in the two direct references which Martin has made to it, I find he is accurate; and a fair inference may be drawn that in other respects his testimony to a matter of fact may be received. Thomas was a Fellow, and Master of Arts, of King's College, Cambridge, and the author of the Dictionary which bears the name of Thomas Thomasius, first published in 1588. He was licensed printer to the University 3 May, 1582, but nothing of his is known before 1584. This was occasioned by the Stationers' Company having, on some plea or other, seized his press. Another license was granted to him Feb. 11, 1584. Strype [Annals 3. 442] has given the following account: "A new press had been set up at Cambridge, and in 1586 the Harmony, translated out of the Latin, was printing there, which for some reasons was not allowed to be printed in London. Whitgift sent his Letter to the Vice-chancellor and

Heads to cause the said book to be stayed from printing;" it was, however, published the same year, and it might be, as Strype says, "after some review or correction of it," for it has " alowed by publique authoritie" in the title-page, and that the " bishops called them in " may be collected from the following entry in the Stationers' Register A, quoted by Herbert, p. 1417, under the year 1589-90, " Whereas all the seiz'd books were sold to Mr. Byshop, be it remembered that 40 of them being Harmonies of the Churches rated at ijs le peece, were had from him by warrant of my Ld. of Cant. and remain at Lambeth, with Mr. Doctor Cosens."

P. 8, l. 20. *Diotrephes his Dialogue*] See another allusion to the same work at p. 16 : " as my friend Tertullus says in the poor Dialogue that the Bishops burned hath lately set down." The title is, " The State of the Church of England laide open in a Conference betweene Diotrephes a Byshoppe, Tertullus a Papiste, Demetrius a Usurer, Pandochus an Innekeeper, and Paul a preacher of the Word of God," printed by Waldegrave, without date, in 1588. *See Note to p.* 30, *l.* 28.

P. 13, l. 18. *Gammer Gurton's Needle*] Martin here is correct when he tells the doctor this is none of his doing. The author was John Still, Bishop of Bath and Wells, and though acted before, " in Christes Colledge Cambridge," is not known to have been printed until 1575. It is reprinted in Collier's Old Plays.

P. 25, l 14. *Tarleton*] Allusion to this celebrated actor and buffoon is frequent in the old dramatists. In 1583 he was chosen one of the Queen's twelve players. He died Sept. 3, 1588. In " A Whip for an Ape, or Martin displaied," 1589, he is thus noticed,—

" Now Tarleton's dead the Consort lacks a vice,
    For knave and fool thou must bear pricke and price : "

and again, in some Rhymes against Martin,—

" These tinkers terms and barbers jests first Tarleton on the stage,
    Then Martin in his bookes of lies, hath put in every page."

P. 29, l. 15. *the Iesuit at Newgate*] probably Edmund Campion, who was executed in 1581, although Whitgift was not " Lord of Canterbury" until 1583.

P. 30, l. 9. *John Wolfe*] Was chosen beadle of the Stationers' Company in 1587. According to Herbert [1170] he was in special favour with the court of assistants, and chosen from his diligence in hunting out and giving intelligence of books disorderly printed. Herbert has given a catalogue of the numerous books printed by and licensed to him.

P. 30, l. 28. *Waldegraue hath left house and home*] An entry in the Register of the Stationers' Company explains the cause of proceeding against him. " May 13, 1588. Whereas Mr. Caldock, warden, Thomas Woodcock, Oliver Wilkes, and John Wolf, on the 16 April last, upon search of Rob. Walgraues house, did seise of his and bring to Stationershall according to the late decrees of the Starre-chamber, and by vertue thereof, a presse with twoo paire of cases with certain Pica Romane, and Pica Italian letters, with diuers books entituled 'The state of the Church of Englande laid open,' &c. For that Walgraue without aucthority and contrary to the said Decrees had printed the said book. Yt is now in full Court, ordered and agreed by force of the said decrees and according to the same, That the said books shall be burnte and the said presse, letters and printing stuffe defaced and made unserviceable." [Herbert, 1145, who gives the Star-Chamber Decrees.] Waldegrave, after this, by the assistance of friends, collected money, and commenced printing at Edinburgh in 1590, being printer to James VI. In that year he brought out the Confession of the Church of Scotland, and on the reverse of the title is the king's patent. [Given by Herbert, 1507.] Until James's accession to the crown of England, in 1603, he remained in Scotland, and then removed to London. The last book which Herbert quotes as being printed by him in Edinburgh is dated in 1600, but in 1602 I find his name to " Cartwright's Answer to the Preface of the Rhemish Testament," printed there in that year.

P. 32, l. 10. *one Thomas Orwin*] " Mar. 4, 1587-8. At a court holden this day yt is ordeyned and decreed that T. Orwyn shall from henceforth leave off from further dealinge with printinge whatsoever till such time as the Master, Wardens, and four of the Court of Assistants shall present his name to the High Commissioners," &c.; which it appears they did, for on the 7th March the Archbishop of Canterbury, the Bishop of London, Dr. Cosin, and Dr. Walker addressed a letter to the Court of Stationers, on which he was elected a printer, and presented 14th May to the Archbishop and others, and admitted the 20th May, 1588, to be a printer according to the said decree. [Stationers' Register, quoted in Herbert.]

P. 32, l. 25. *For Reignolds the papist at Rheimes in his booke against M. Whitakers*] The first Roman Catholic translation of the New Testament into English, was printed by John Fogny, at Rheims, in 1582, to which Whitaker replied in the same year, and was answered by W. Rainoldes in " A Refutation of sundry Reprehensions, Cavils and false Sleightes, by which M. Whitaker laboureth to deface the late English translation, and Catholike annotations of the New Testament, and the Booke of the Discovery of heretical Corruptions. Paris, 1583," in 12mo. To this Whitaker then rejoined in " An Answer to W. Rainolds' Refutation of Sundry Reprehensions," &c., 1585, in 8vo.

P. 35, l. 26. *If suche another booke as the Ecclesiast. Discipline*] Strype [Annals, iii. 285] has given us the following account of this work. " The Brief and Plain Declaration was written in Latin in 1574, and reprinted in English 1584. It seemed to be printed beyond sea. [ed. 1584.] Travers, I think, was the author. The Epistle commendatory is T. Cartwright's," and the reason why it was written in Latin, he says, was that it might be read by the Queen, " who was delighted with things written in Latin." Bancroft, who lived at the time, has given us a more particular account in his " Survey of the Pretended Holy Discipline," and in his " Dangerous Positions," both printed in 1593. About the year 1583, where before the platforme of Geneva (for it was left at large in Cartwright's books) had been followed, now there was a particular draught made for England, with a new form of common prayer therein prescribed. It was published the following year, but there were found some imperfections in it, which were referred to Travers to be corrected by him; and being performed, it came out again in 1586, but it was then severed from the book of common prayer. About Sturbridge fair time, in 1589, another synod, or general meeting, was held in St. John's College, Cambridge, where some other corrections and additions were made, after which those present voluntarily agreed to subscribe it. [See Bancroft's Survey, 66, and Dangerous Positions, 68, 89.] Neal, under the year 1584, states, that " whilst printing at Cambridge, it was seized at the press; the Archbishop advised that all the copies should be burnt as factious and seditious, but one was found in Mr. Cartwright's study after his death, and reprinted in 1644." [Neal, i. 358.]

P. 36, l. 22. *the Confutation of the Rhemish Testament may be published*] Clark, in his Life of Cartwright, tells us, that on the publication of the New Testament at Rheims, Queen Elizabeth sent to Beza, requesting him to answer it. Beza replied, that she had one in her own kingdom far abler than he was to perform such a work, mentioning Cartwright. In the preface to the Confutation, first printed in 1618, we have the following account: "The first remarkable motive it seemeth came from Sir F. Walsingham, who herein as in other affaires, was accounted the mouth and hand of the late Queen and State, by whom M. Cartwright was not onely incited to begin this busines, but assured also of such aid as should be necessarie for the finishing thereof, to which purpose he sent him an hundred pounds towards the charges, which buying of books and procuring of writers was like to bring upon him. This was about the year 1583, as appeareth by the date of M. Cartwright's letters in answer of the aforesaid motive, which testifie also of the receipt of that hundred pounds." Being also earnestly solicited by several eminent divines of Cambridge, as well as the ministers of London and Suffolk, Cartwright begun the work, and had made considerable progress, when "thorough the envious opposition of some potent adversaries, he met with so great discouragement and hinderances, that he was moved oftimes to lay pen aside, as appears by the letter of 1586 to a noble Earle and Privie Councellor of great note in answer of a letter to encourage him in the work and to understand the forwardness thereof, and by another of 1590, wherein he certifieth the said Earle that about four years before he had received commandment from the archbishop that then was [Whitgift] to deal no further in it, and yet upon special solicitation and encouragements both by him and some other honorable personages he had at last taken pen in hand againe;" but, receiving new discouragements from his great adversaries, together with his continual employment in the ministry, he was prevented from finishing it. The copy remained for 30 years in MS., and had become somewhat eaten by mice, so that, as published in 1618, the missing parts, and all after Revelations xv., are completed from Fulke's work on the same subject. Pierce, in his Vindication, hints that Queen Elizabeth furnished the money that Walsingham sent to him; but if she had done so, the Archbishop would hardly have interfered in opposition to her will.

P. 43, l. 22. *There was the last sommer a little catechisme, made by M. Davison*] Herbert, in quoting the title, [p. 1588,] refers to Maunsell's Catalogue, p. 29; but a copy was in Heber's collection,

[Bib. Heber. ii. p. 25,] the title of which is, "A short Christian Institution made first for the use of a private family, and now communicated by the Author to other Flocks and Families, by J. D.," printed by R. Waldegrave, without date, in 1588.

P. 47, l. 24. *that no Byble should be bounde without the Apocripha*] Fuller [Ch. Hist. bk. ix.] states, that amongst other things discussed at the assemblies of the Puritans was the question, " Whether the books called Apocryphal were warrantable to be read publicly in the church as the canonical Scripture?" but it must be evident to those who are acquainted with their history, that they rejected the whole as uncanonical. In 1588 Martin denounces it as an attempt to mingle heaven and earth together. In 1592 we find the following language in a Petition to her Majesty: "Sundrie of the Prelates do preach and take their texts out of the Apocrypha, wherein they go beyond their commission, unlesse the Apocrypha be a part of Scripture, as one of the Bishops doth entitle it." [Petition, &c., 66.] In 1604 we find, from the Apology of the Lincolnshire Ministers, that one of their objections to the Book of Common Prayer was because " It does too much honour to the Apocryphal writings, commanding many of them to be read for first lessons under the name of Holy Scripture."

P. 54, l. 29. *O well bowlde, when Iohn of London throwes his bowle*] An allusion to the favourite amusement of Bishop Aylmer. For further particulars the reader is referred to Strype's Life of Aylmer.

P. 55, l. 22. *olde Doctor Turner*] Probably Dr. William Turner, author of the English Herbal, a New Book of Spiritual Physik, and other works.

THE END.

LONDON:
GILBERT AND RIVINGTON, PRINTERS, ST. JOHN'S SQUARE.